# THE 40 PARABLES OF INVESTING

### Decoding the Hidden Investing Secrets in the Parables

## MIKE NACH

Copyright © 2014 Mike Nach

**All rights reserved.** No part of this book may be reproduced in whole or in part without written permission from the publisher, except by reviewers who may quote brief excerpts in connection with a review in a newspaper, magazine, or electronic publication; nor may any part of the book be reproduced, stored in a retrieval system, or transmitted in any form by means electronic, mechanical, photocopying, recording, or other, without written permission from the publisher.

ISBN-13: 978-1502700988
ISBN-10: 1502700980

# Table of Contents

Disclaimer ................................................................................. 1
Introduction ............................................................................. 3
Love of Money .......................................................................... 9
1- Don't Be Greedy ................................................................ 11
2- Don't Stash your Cash, Invest it ....................................... 17
3- It is Never Too Late to Start Investing ............................ 21
4- Create a Cash Cushion ..................................................... 25
5- Start Small ......................................................................... 29
6- If You Are Certain About the Outcome, Then Put All Your Eggs in One Basket ................................................................ 31
7- Be a Value Investor .......................................................... 33
8- Act like an Owner ............................................................. 35
9- Passive Investor ................................................................ 39
10- Small Cap Stocks ............................................................. 43
11- Stocks of Great Companies ............................................. 45
12- Companies with Strong Foundations ............................ 47
13- Brand Names ................................................................... 51
14- Shareholder Friendly Companies .................................. 53
15- Four Types of Companies ............................................... 55
16- Stock Market Cycles ....................................................... 59
17- The Stock Market Is Unpredictable .............................. 63
18- Sell I ................................................................................. 65
19- Sell II ............................................................................... 67
20- Exit a Losing Trade ........................................................ 69
21- Averaging Down and Derivatives ................................. 71
22- Adapt or Perish ............................................................... 73

23- Be On Guard ................................................................ 77
24- Be Alert ...................................................................... 79
25- Don't Be Overconfident ............................................. 81
26- Don't Be Reckless ...................................................... 83
27- Control Your Emotions ............................................. 87
28- Don't Panic! ............................................................... 91
29- Check on Your Investments ..................................... 95
30- Missing Stocks and Money ....................................... 97
31- Track Your Expenses ............................................... 101
32- Do Your Taxes I ....................................................... 105
33- Do Your Taxes II ..................................................... 107
34- Rumors and Tips ..................................................... 111
35- Fake Stock Market Gurus I ..................................... 115
36- Fake Stock Market Gurus II ................................... 117
37- Beware of Scam Artists .......................................... 119
38- Trust No One ........................................................... 125
39- Unscrupulous Brokers and Financial Advisors ... 127
40- The Internet Is Your Friend .................................... 133
Summary ......................................................................... 135
Thank You! ..................................................................... 143
My Books ........................................................................ 144

# Disclaimer

The author has used his best efforts in preparing this book. Every effort has been made to accurately represent the teachings / techniques mentioned in this book, and their potential. The author has no investments in the stocks of companies mentioned in this book.

Stocks, futures, options and derivatives trading are not appropriate for everyone. There is a substantial risk of loss associated with trading these markets. Losses can and will occur. Never invest any money that you cannot safely afford to lose. No system or methodology has ever been developed that can guarantee profits or ensure freedom from losses. No representation or implication is being made that using this methodology or system or the information in this book will generate profits or ensure freedom from losses.

Because this book is published for multiple readers, it cannot possibly take into account the investment objectives, financial situation, or specific needs of any individual. Accordingly, before acting on any of the recommendations provided in this book, you must first make certain they are appropriate to your specific investment needs, objectives, or financial circumstances. Consulting a competent professional is advisable.

The author and publisher shall in no event be held liable to any party for any direct, indirect, punitive, special, psychological, religious, spiritual, monetary, incidental or other consequential damages arising, directly or indirectly, from any use of this material, which is provided "as is", and without warranties.

If you wish to apply the ideas contained in this book, you are taking full responsibility for your action.

# Introduction

Two thousand years ago, Jesus, the greatest teacher of all time, bequeathed us the priceless parables. Even today, his parables still astound us with their timeless and extraordinary truths.

What is a parable?

A parable is a word-picture which uses an image or story to help the listener to discover the deeper meaning and underlying truth of the reality being portrayed. Jesus was a master storyteller. He loved to use illustrations and comparisons to teach his listeners awesome truths. Jesus' parables comprise more than one-third of his teachings. These parables have been called "heavenly stories with earthly meanings," or "earthly stories with heavenly meanings." They contain some of the most profound yet easy to understand lessons taught by the master.

To start with, Jesus' parables are among the most powerful teachings in Western civilization!

The parables of Jesus will enlighten you if you approach them with an open mind and heart, ready to let them challenge you. When reading the parables it's important to not get bogged down in the details of the story. Focus on the main idea.

If you approach the parables and the interpretations with the conviction that you already know the answer, you will be looking but not seeing, listening but not hearing.

Can we connect the 2000 year old parables with the modern world of investing?

You will be surprised! Jesus structured his parables in a way that their teachings are relevant even today. A very careful reading and study of the parables will help you decode the hidden meanings in the parables to invest wisely; be debt free; make correct decisions and see your family and your business prosper. You will be intrigued how well the parables fit in with the modern world of investing.

Don't be a skeptic. Don't be a critic. Don't shout out that Jesus did not intend the parables to be used for making money. Have an open mind. Brace yourself. Read what Jesus had to say in the parable **"Ten Servants and Minas."** He spoke about the need to investing money and making it grow! Jesus was against greed not money. He despised people who made money cheating others like the moneychangers at the Jewish temple. I guess Jesus wouldn't want you to be poor. He wants you to be rich the right way. Be rich ethically. And trust me; poverty is not a virtue to be embraced.

This book is for the novice as also the most sophisticated investor. It's not necessary to know lots of sophisticated techniques or financial jargon to be an astute investor.

If you apply the simple principles of the parables you will build substantial wealth for you and your family.

Here's a preview of what is on offer in this book-

**1: The Rich Young Man-** What is the first deadly sin of investing?

**2: Ten Servants and Minas-** Do you stash your cash under the mattress?

**3: The Workers in the Vineyard-** Can a late bloomer strike it rich in the stock market?

**4: The Ten Virgins-** Are you unprepared like the foolish virgins?

**5: Lowest Seat at a Feast-** The first step?

**6: Hidden Treasure and Priceless Pearl-** What if you discovered a sure-fire winner stock?

**7: The Eagles and the Carcass-** Who is an eagle and what is the carcass?

**8: Faithful and Wise Servant-** What should you, as a company shareholder or mutual fund investor, be aware of?

**9: The Shepherd and His Flock-** Are you a passive investor?

**10: The Growing Seed-** Which stocks can grow your wealth over a period of time?

**11: The Ten Lepers-** Why you must have faith and patience with your stock picks?

**12: The Wise and Foolish Builders-** What are the characteristics of companies with strong foundations?

**13: Lamp on a Stand-** Which companies do not remain hidden for long?

**14: The Two Debtors-** Why do shareholders stick with some companies?

**15: Four Types of Soil-** How to identify the characteristics of your company before taking an investment decision?

**16: Lazarus and the Rich Man-** What is a market cycle?

**17: The Weather Signs-** What is the main danger of the stock market?

**18: The Sheep and the Goats-** How will you deal with an investment or a stock that has not fulfilled your investment objectives?

**19: The Barren Fig Tree-** Do you suffer from loss aversion bias?

**20: The Two Sons-** What if you have made a mistake?

**21: The Evil Tenants of the Vineyard-** Who are the evil tenants of the vineyard?

**22: Old Cloth and New Wine / Wineskins-** Why "patching up" could be a mistake?

**23: Watchfulness-** Are you vigilant enough to protect your investments?

**24: Signs from a Fig Tree-** How to deal with uncertainties in the stock market?

**25: Master and Servant-** What are the hallmarks of a wise and successful investor?

**26: The Rich Fool-** Do you relate with the rich fool?

**27: The Great Banquet-** What to do if your position goes against you?

**28: The Weeds-** How to deal with panic selling situations?

**29: The Fishing Net-** How do I maintain a healthy portfolio?

**30: The Lost Sheep, Lost Coin-** Want to know how to track down your missing or unclaimed money, stocks, IRS tax refunds, Pension and Life insurance etc.?

**31: The Cost of Being a Disciple-** Why you should invest within your means?

**32: The Pharisee and the Tax Collector-** What is common between Mr. Market and Mr. IRS?

**33: What Defiles a Person-** What defiles a market participant?

**34: The Doctor and the Sick-** How to minimize your tax burden?

**35: The Blind Leading the Blind-** Why should you avoid stock market pundits?

**36: The Shrewd Manager-** What action you need to take if you think you have been ripped by your broker, advisor or a scam artist?

**37: The Unmerciful Servant-** How to take action against unscrupulous brokers, scam artists or advisors who have been ripping you off?

**38: The Good Samaritan-** Who are the Good Samaritans?

**39: The Tree and Its Fruits-** Who are the false prophets of the markets?

**40: Friend in Need-** Who is your friend who will help and advise you 24/7 without a word of protest?

There's tons of information in these pages. I urge you to read this book, page by page and study each parable, the accompanying interpretations and bottom lines carefully. Give serious consideration to the lessons and your life will never be the same again.

Practice what the parables preach.

**You will be an enlightened investor!**

# Love of Money

**1Timothy 6:10**: "**For the love of money is the root of all evil: which while some coveted after, they have erred from the faith, and pierced themselves through with many sorrows.**"

The Apostle Paul had this to say, in his first letter, to his young disciple, Timothy. This verse has often been misquoted as saying, "Money is the root of all evil." Notice how "money" is substituted for "love of money." This change, while subtle, alters the meaning of the verse. The misquoted version ("money is the root of all evil") makes money and wealth the source (or root) of all evil in the world.

**It's the love of money or greed that's the root of all evil!**

# 1- Don't Be Greedy

## The Rich Young Man

### Mark 10:25

It is easier for a camel to go through the eye of a needle, than for a rich man to enter into the kingdom of God.

**Interpretation:**

What did Jesus mean when he said the above words?

Read what the Apostle Paul wrote to his young disciple, Timothy, "For *the love of money is the root of all evil:* which while some coveted after, they have erred from the faith, and pierced themselves through with many sorrows." (**1Timothy 6:10**)

Now, let's visualize Jerusalem during the time of the New Testament. The Passover of the Jews was at hand. Jesus enters the temple and finds peddlers selling oxen, sheep and pigeons for worship and sacrifice, at exorbitant prices. Since Jerusalem was under Roman occupation, Roman money was in common use. The Jewish authorities did not consider the Roman coins, with the image of a pagan emperor, acceptable to God. So, when Jews came to pay their Temple tax, they could only pay it with a special Hebrew coin, the half-shekel.

Enter the moneychangers. They were allowed to set up tables and benches for themselves in the Temple where they exchanged not just local Roman money, but also foreign currency from distant travelers, for shekels. Unfortunately, the shekels were not plentiful and the money changers had cornered the shekel market.

Thus, they were able to raise the exchange rates to whatever the market could bear. They used their monopoly they had on these coins to make exorbitant profits, forcing the Jews to pay whatever these money changers demanded.

Jesus notices the greed prevailing in the house of God and loses his cool. Making a whip of cords, he drives them all out of the temple, with the pigeons, sheep and oxen. He tosses out the coins of the money-changers and overturns their tables (**Matthew 21:12, John 2:13-16**). See the picture?

The above verses have often been misinterpreted as "money is the root of all evil," "rich guys don't go to heaven" and "Jesus was anti-business." We are missing the main point here.

Let's add some phrases in Jesus' parable and his message will be clear. *"It is easier for a camel to go through the eye of a needle, than for a rich man **(if he is greedy)** to enter into the kingdom of God **(lead a peaceful life)**."* Makes sense?

What is the common thread in the above paragraphs? It's greed!

Greed or **Love of Money** - perhaps more than anything else in our world- has led to wars and financial bubbles over the centuries.

Money has become the fall guy. It is not evil. It is simply a medium of exchange.

Money was not the primary cause of the **Dotcom Crash of 2000-2002**. It was pure greed. At the time investors leaped at any investment opportunity which had a '.com' at the end of it. There was frenzied buying activity in internet-related stocks, many just start-ups with no business plans or earnings forecasts. Investors got greedy. Everybody wanted a piece of the next Microsoft. These junk grade stocks were ramped up and became terribly overpriced. Eventually this created a bubble which burst in mid-2000 keeping the stock market depressed through 2002.

It was greed which led to the **Housing Bubble and Credit Crisis (2007-2009)**. In order to avoid the economy from going into a recession the Federal Reserve cut interest rates. The banks grabbed this cheap money and started doling out loans to all and sundry. At this time, the housing market was moving upwards. People were buying more than one home and everybody felt that the prices would go up and up. Individuals who could not afford to pay off the mortgages also wanted to buy houses. Loans were given to these people, too.

These loans were bought and bundled by the banks into **mortgage backed securities (MBS)**. The banks were also making money on the fees associated with the process and not on holding the MBS themselves. These securities were sold to financial institutions and eager investors who were pleased with their high rates of return. The ratings agencies did not understand the nature of these securities but they handed out AAA ratings on these junk grade securities.

The home prices peaked and the prices started falling. It became difficult for borrowers to refinance their homes. Mortgage delinquencies soared and families lost their money. Securities backed with mortgages, including subprime mortgages, widely held by global firms, lost most of their value.

The crisis wiped out much of the capital of the global banks. In the US, the government had to bail out the banks who were involved in this mess, with hundreds of billions of taxpayer's money. Stock markets crashed and ……..

If the Feds, like Jesus, had taken timely action, the crisis could have been aborted at the initial stages itself.

Oh! Let's not forget **Bernie Madoff**. He swindled billions of dollars from unwary investors, including billionaires and celebrities, over the course of nearly two decades. He's also serving a 150 year sentence for his greed.

There you are! Greed does not pay. Want to know whether you are greedy?

You are greedy if you-

**1: Buy on hot tips and rumors-** Greed compels us to buy or sell a particular stock based on a hot tip or rumor. Most of these rumors benefit the source of information and you will be left with losses.

**2: Buy in a rising market-** In a rising or bull market, everybody wants to pile on the bandwagon and buy stocks when their prices are rising. Greed is the culprit here. Finally, when the trend reverses and prices start falling, there's nobody to bail you out.

**3: Buy get-rich-schemes from internet scam artists-** Did you ever fall a prey to get-rich-quick schemes advertised in unsolicited emails, phone calls or letters? Nigerian money scams? Why would a complete stranger offer to make you awesomely rich for a few dollars? Would he not keep the "awesome secret" for himself and become a billionaire?

**4: Trade derivatives-** The world's greatest investor, **Warren Buffett**, termed derivatives as "Weapons of Mass Destruction." They are precisely that. 95% of derivatives traders lose all their money and are soon out of the market. Don't listen if somebody tells you that trading in derivatives will be your gateway to riches.

**Bottom Line:**

Greed is not good. You don't need to be greedy to be rich. Have a balanced approach while investing.

# 2- Don't Stash your Cash, Invest it

## Ten Servants and Minas

### Luke 19:11-27

A man of noble birth went to a distant country to have himself appointed king and then to return. So he called ten of his servants and gave them ten minas. "Put this money to work," he said, "until I come back."

But his subjects hated him and sent a delegation after him to say, "We don't want this man to be our king." He was made king, however, and returned home.

Then he sent for the servants to whom he had given the money, in order to find out what they had gained with it.

The first one came and said, "Sir, your mina has earned ten more."

His master was pleased and replied, "Well done, my good servant! Because you have been trustworthy in a very small matter, take charge of ten cities."

The second came and said, "Sir, your mina has earned five more."

His master answered, "You take charge of five cities."

Then another servant came and said, "Sir, here is your mina. I have kept it laid away in a piece of cloth. I was afraid of you, because you are a hard man. You take out what you did not put in and reap what you did not sow."

His master replied, "I will judge you by your own words, you wicked servant! You knew, did you, that I am a hard man, taking out what I did not put in, and reaping what I did not sow? Why then didn't you put my money on deposit, so that when I came back, I could have collected it with interest?"

Then he said to those standing by, "Take his mina away from him and give it to the one who has ten minas."

They protested, "Sir, he already has ten!"

He replied, "I tell you that to everyone who has, more will be given, but as for the one who has nothing, even what he has will be taken away. But those enemies of mine who did not want me to be king over them—bring them here and kill them in front of me."

**Interpretation:**

Do you stash your cash under the mattress?

Has your fear of losing your money prevented you from investing and doing what is needed to increase your wealth?

Are you aware that inflation is eroding your nest egg?

Huh?

Look at it this way.

Let's suppose you stashed away $10,000 under the mattress in July 1994. In June 2014 you realized that you need it for your kid's college expenses and take it out. You will be shocked to know that the value of your $10,000 is now only $6,230! Are you kidding me? No! The termites did not eat your cash. A 60.5% cumulative rate of inflation did! (Check out this inflation calculator **http://www.usinflationcalculator.com/**) During the same period the total price return of the S&P 500 (if you had reinvested all of your dividends) would have been 279.582% (adjusted for inflation). (This site is for S&P 5000 returns **http://dqydj.net/sp-500-return-calculator/**)

The S&P 500 has outraced inflation!

Most people fear that if they invested their money in stocks they would lose it all. There is some truth in their feelings. Yes! If you bought a dud stock or invested at peak prices you could lose your nest egg.

If you want to play it safe, you can protect your purchasing power and investment returns (over the long run) by investing in a number of inflation-protected securities such as **inflation-indexed bonds** or **Treasury Inflation-Protected Securities (TIPS)**.

**TIPS:** Treasury Inflation-Protected Securities, or TIPS, provide protection against inflation. The principal of a TIPS increases with inflation and decreases with deflation, as measured by the Consumer Price Index. When a TIPS matures, you are paid the adjusted principal or original principal, whichever is greater. TIPS pay interest twice a year, at a fixed rate. The rate is applied to the adjusted principal; so, like the principal, interest payments rise with inflation and fall with deflation.

These types of investments move with inflation and therefore are immune to inflation risk.

**Bottom Line:**

**1:** If you leave your money under the mattress, over a period of time, your money will lose its value to inflation.

**2:** During the past 50 years, through many ups and downs, the average large stock has returned close to 10% a year -- well ahead of inflation, bonds, gold, real estate and other savings vehicles.

**3:** Stocks are the best way to save money for long-term goals like retirement and children's college funds.

**4:** If you want to play it safe, invest in inflation-indexed bonds that move with inflation and therefore, immune to inflation risk.

# 3- It is Never Too Late to Start Investing

## The Workers in the Vineyard

### Matthew 20:1-16

The kingdom of heaven is like a landowner who went out early in the morning to hire men to work in his vineyard. He agreed to pay them a denarius for the day and sent them into his vineyard. About the third hour he went out and saw others standing in the marketplace doing nothing. He told them, "You also go and work in my vineyard, and I will pay you whatever is right." So they went.

He went out again about the sixth hour and the ninth hour and did the same thing. About the eleventh hour, he went out and found still others standing around. He asked them, "Why have you been standing here all day long doing nothing?" They answered, "No one has hired us." He said to them, "You also go and work in my vineyard."

When evening came, the owner of the vineyard said to his foreman, "Call the workers and pay them their wages, beginning with the last ones hired and going onto the first."

The workers who were hired about the eleventh hour came and each received a denarius. The workers, who were hired first, noticed this and they expected to receive more. But each one of them also received a denarius.

When they received it, they began to grumble against the landowner.

"These men who were hired last worked only one hour," they said, "and you have made them equal to us who have borne the burden of the work and the heat of the day."

But he answered one of them, "Friend, I am not being unfair to you. Didn't you agree to work for a denarius? Take your pay and go. I want to give the man who was hired last the same as I gave you. Don't I have the right to do what I want with my own money? Or are you envious because I am generous? So, the last will be first, and the first will be last."

**Interpretation:**

In the above parable, the guys who came in very late also got the same rewards as those who toiled from morning. The stock market is a place where an investor who has entered late can with one home run investment (like buying **Tesla** or **Netflix** shares) beat those who were in the game for years. It's never too late to invest in the stock market. It's not the holding period that makes you rich. It's what you buy and at what price which can make you super wealthy.

Suppose you have never given a thought to investing during your active years and now you want to jump in. A late bloomer could start with-

**Start with a 401k**: If you have one, you can start with this as you begin to ramp up your investing. The contribution limit for 2014 is $17,500. If you are over 50 you are eligible for a catch up contribution of $5,500. The employer contribution doesn't count towards that limit, so take advantage of all the free money you can. Remember, the combined contribution limit is $51,000. Go ahead, start with your 401k and begin with the lowest funds possible.

**Open an IRA**: After 401k, you should open an IRA. You may be limited in your ability to make a tax-deferred contribution. Speak with a tax advisor about this aspect. Check out what are your options for funding an IRA and get started on it.

**Educate yourself and be optimistic**: It's never too late to invest in the stock market. If you learn the basics of investing you can do as well as a guy who has been investing for years.

**Bottom Line:**

**1:** It's the quality of the stock and the price you buy it that determines whether you will be very rich or not. With one home run investment you can become rich very quickly. You could beat the guys who have been holding on to mediocre stocks for years.

**2:** If you bought 8 Tesla Motors shares for $987.44 on Jun 29, 2013 and held it till Jul 15, 2014 the value would be $ 1,756.66 (67.39% returns).

Similarly if you bought 4 shares of Netflix for $987.44 on Jun 29, 2013 and held it till Jul 15, 2014, the value would be $1,985.54 (119.46% returns). Can you beat that? It's not necessary to be early in the game; it's how you play it!

**3:** If you have woken up like Rip Van Winkle and need to invest safely, start with 401K and open an IRA account.

# 4- Create a Cash Cushion

## The Ten Virgins

### Matthew 25:1-13

There were ten virgins who took their lamps and went out to meet the bridegroom. Five of them were foolish and five were wise. The foolish ones took their lamps but did not take any oil with them. The wise, however, took oil in jars along with their lamps. The bridegroom was a long time in coming, and they all became drowsy and fell asleep.

At midnight the cry rang out, "Here's the bridegroom! Come out to meet him!" Then all the virgins woke up and trimmed their lamps.

The foolish ones said to the wise, "Give us some of your oil; our lamps are going out."

"No," they replied, "there may not be enough for both us and you. Instead, go to those who sell oil and buy some for yourselves."

But while they were on their way to buy the oil, the bridegroom arrived. The virgins who were ready went in with him to the wedding banquet. And the door was shut.

Later the others also came. "Sir!" they yelled. "Open the door for us!"

But he replied, "Who are you? I don't know you."

Therefore keep watch, because you do not know the day or the hour.'

**Interpretation:**

In the above parable the foolish virgins did not have oil when their lamps were about to go out. No cushion when the lamps burned out. Don't be like the foolish virgins.

Companies making too many sales have also gone bankrupt when they failed to maintain positive cash flows. How? If a company spends its money to make the sales but don't get paid until months later, it will have no money to continue running the business. The companies should make sure that they have money coming in as fast as it is going out to meet expenses. Otherwise there will be no oil in the lamp.

If you are an individual investor, have cash on hand. Don't spend it all. If you have a cushion of cash, it can help you stay invested when stocks fall — as they surely will sooner or later. And your cash hoard can enable you to do what cash-poor investors find almost impossible: Buying stocks at bargain prices during the market lows or bearish periods.

**Bottom Line:**

How much cash should you hold in your portfolio? It really depends on who you are, what's your investing style and your investment horizon. I recommend 5 to 10 percent. It will help buy you great stocks at bargain prices during the bearish phase.

# 5- Start Small

## Lowest Seat at a Feast

### Luke 14:7-14

When Jesus noticed how the guests chose the places of honor at the table, he told them this parable: When you are invited by someone to a wedding feast, do not take the place of honor, for a person more distinguished than you may have been invited. If so, the host who invited both of you will come and say, "Give your place to this person." Then, embarrassedly you will have to take the least important place. But when you are invited, go and sit in the lowest place, so that when your host comes, he will say to you, "Friend, move up to a better place." Then you will be honored in the presence of all your fellow guests. For everyone who are proud will be humbled and he who is humble will be exalted. Also, remember, when you give a luncheon or dinner, do not invite your friends, your brothers or relatives, or your rich neighbors; if you do, they may invite you back and so you will be repaid. But when you give a banquet, invite the poor, the crippled, the lame, the blind, and you will be blessed. Although they cannot repay you, you will be repaid at the resurrection of the righteous.

**Interpretation:**

There will always be ups and downs in the stock market.

While investing, it is advisable to start small and if your position turns profitable, scale up. It is also easier to exit a loss making investment when your investment is small.

Sorry, Jesus! Hey, guys! Don't ever invest in poor, crippled, lame or blind companies. They are not going to bless you. Invest in good, healthy companies.

**Bottom Line:**

Start small. After your position turns profitable, scale up.

# 6- If You Are Certain About the Outcome, Then Put All Your Eggs in One Basket

## Hidden Treasure and Priceless Pearl

### Matthew 13:44-46

The kingdom of heaven is like treasure hidden in a field. When a man found it, he hid it again, and then in his joy went and sold all he had and bought that field.

Again, the kingdom of heaven is like a merchant looking for fine pearls. When he found one of great value, he went away and sold everything he had and bought it.

**Interpretation:**

Most stock market gurus advise you not to put all your eggs in one basket. There's some truth behind it. Diversifying your portfolio helps mitigate your risk. Diversified investments hedge against each other and limit your losses if a part of the stocks in your portfolio perform badly.

But, what if you discovered or got sure-fire information that a particular stock will shoot up soon?

Follow Jesus' advice- Sell off your existing investments and with the cash buy this stock as much as you can and wait.

It is risky but worth a try, if you are sure of your bet.

**Bottom Line:**

If you figured (don't include dreams or hunches) that a particular stock will generate spectacular returns, buy this stock as much as you can.

Have a stop loss so that you can bail out with a small loss if you are wrong. This strategy requires courage. It's also the reason why some people become very rich. These people are ready to stake everything they got when they are sure of a profit. It can also make you poor. It works both ways.

Do not adapt this strategy while trading derivatives. Derivatives are highly leveraged products. You will lose a great deal if your position goes against you.

# 7- Be a Value Investor

## The Eagles and the Carcass

### Luke 17:37, Matthew 24:28

And they said to him, "Where, Lord?" He said to them, "Where the body is, there the eagles will be gathered together."

**Interpretation:**

The body or carcass is the battered stocks in a bear market and the eagles are the value investors waiting to grab good stocks at bargain prices.

**Bottom Line:**

**1:** Be a value investor. Buy when the market is littered with battered stocks of good companies and when everybody is selling at bargain prices.

**2:** Listen to Warren Buffett's sage advice- 'I will tell you how to become rich. Be fearful when others are greedy. Be greedy when others are fearful.'

# 8- Act like an Owner

## Faithful and Wise Servant

### Matthew 24:45-51, Luke 12:42-48

A faithful, sensible servant is one to whom the master can give the responsibility of managing his other household servants and feeding them. If the master returns and finds that the servant has done a good job, there will be a reward. Assuredly, the master will put that servant in charge of all he owns.

But what if the servant thinks, "My master won't be back for a while" and he begins beating the other servants, partying, and getting drunk? The master will return unannounced and unexpected, and he will punish or fire him.

And a servant who knows what the master wants, but isn't prepared and doesn't carry out those instructions, will be severely punished. But someone who does not know, and then does something wrong, will be punished only lightly. When someone has been given much, much will be required in return and when someone has been entrusted with much, even more will be required.

**Interpretation:**

**Who are the masters and servants in a company?**

The masters of a company are the owners, investors or shareholders of the company. The Board of Directors, managers and other employees are the servants. It's the duty of the servants to run the company well and reward its masters.

The top management of a company is paid huge salaries and stock options to run a company well. They should be aware that their corporate action has an effect over the company's stock price. Their performance should justify their pay benefits.

The company should also reward the managers according to their performance. Companies with highly paid executives and poor performance will be punished with low stock prices. Such executives should be fired.

**What about a mutual fund or a hedge fund?**

The masters of the mutual fund or the hedge fund are its investors. The Board of Directors or Board of Trustees, fund managers and other employees are the servants. They have been entrusted with the responsibility of managing the investor's funds and making it grow. The fund manager should be prepared for market downturns and take preventive action immediately. If they fail to weed out the loss making investments in their fund then the value of their fund will definitely slide. If the fund manager has not been doing this then he should be on the way out.

**Bottom Line:**

**1:** A shareholder is a part owner of the company or mutual fund and this gives them certain rights like voting power on major issues, the right to sue for wrongful acts of the management and entitlement to dividends.

**2:** Shareholders can vote by means of proxy to have a say in the business operations of their company. Shareholders need not attend an important meeting in person to participate in the voting process. They certainly must make the effort to read and understand legal resolutions and vote correctly.

**3:** Investors in a mutual fund like common stockholders can also vote for changes to the board of directors, approve or reject an investment advisor or fund manager, vote for or against changes to a fund's investment objectives, or vote on sales charge modifications.

**4:** Don't be a passive investor.

# 9- Passive Investor

## The Shepherd and His Flock

### John 10:1-18

The man who does not enter the sheep pen by the gate, but climbs in by some other way, is a thief and a robber. The man who enters by the gate is the shepherd of his sheep. The watchman opens the gate for him, and the sheep listen to his voice. He calls his own sheep by name and leads them out.

When he has brought out all his own, he goes on ahead of them, and his sheep follow him because they know his voice. But they will never follow a stranger; in fact, they will run away from him because they do not recognize a stranger's voice. Jesus used this figure of speech, but they did not understand what he was telling them.

I tell you the truth; I am the gate for the sheep.

All who ever came before me were thieves and robbers, but the sheep did not listen to them. I am the gate; whoever enters through me will be saved. He will come in and go out, and find pasture. The thief comes only to steal and kill and destroy; I have come that they may have life, and have it to the full.

I am the good shepherd. The good shepherd lays down his life for the sheep. The hired hand is not the shepherd who owns the sheep. So when he sees the wolf coming, he abandons the sheep and runs away. Then the wolf attacks the flock and scatters it. The man runs away because he is a hired hand and cares nothing for the sheep.

I am the good shepherd; I know my sheep and my sheep know me just as the Father knows me and I know the Father—and I lay down my life for the sheep. I have other sheep that are not of this sheep pen. I must bring them also. They too will listen to my voice, and there shall be one flock and one shepherd. The reason my Father loves me is that I lay down my life—only to take it up again. No one takes it from me, but I lay it down of my own accord. I have authority to lay it down and authority to take it up again. This command I received from my Father.'

**Interpretation:**

If executives have a stake in a company, they will act responsibly. Their wealth is at stake if they don't. If a company is managed by professional managers they should be rewarded (stock options?) for achieving their performance targets. If you need a good shepherd he should own his goats. Why would hired hands lay down their lives if a wolf attacks the flock? They have nothing to lose!

What good is a company if the managers jump ship during adverse business conditions? How reliable are the professional managers of the company? Are there company hoppers among them? Check out their background. If rats run a ship, don't board it.

If you are an investor, don't leave your finances entirely in the hands of your broker or financial advisor. They have nothing to lose if the investment plans go awry. They will collect their commissions and fees irrespective of their performance. Brokers are also known to churn portfolios to earn commissions for their firm. There are many mutual fund and hedge fund managers who also churn out the fund portfolios in search of quick profits. Analyze their actions and figure out the effect on your investment.

**Bottom Line:**

Don't be a passive investor. You might be taken for a ride by brokers, financial advisors, mutual fund and hedge fund managers who are more interested in collecting their fees and commissions rather than improving the performance of the portfolio under their care.

# 10- Small Cap Stocks

## The Growing Seed

### Matthew 13:31-32

The kingdom of God is as if a man should scatter mustard seed on the ground, and should sleep by night and rise by day, and the seed should sprout and grow, he himself does not know how. This seed is the least of all seeds, but when it is grown, it is the greatest among herbs, and becomes a tree, so that the birds of the air come and lodge in its branches.

**Interpretation:**

What does Jesus mean when he says, "The mustard seed is the least of all seeds, but when it is grown, it is the greatest among herbs and becomes a tree?" Can you relate this allegory to stocks?

Think small cap stocks! I am not going to talk about penny stocks, even though they may be the least of all seeds (stocks), because they are riskier and not often traded on the major stock exchanges.

Sometimes, buying small cap stocks- those with market caps of between $ 300 million and $ 2 billion- is more profitable than buying large cap stocks. Over a long period of time, small cap stocks have increased in value faster than the large caps.

Small caps have several advantages over large caps such as being more nimble than larger companies; huge growth potential; thinly traded; being attractive acquisition targets; lack of institutional interest or not having many analysts cover the stock. For the astute investor, these factors can actually present a great deal of opportunity, if they slip in the door early.

Over a period of time, some of these small caps grow into great large cap companies. Did you know that one in eight small-cap growth stocks becomes large every year?

**Bottom Line:**

**1:** Historically, small caps have outperformed the large caps over long periods of time.

**2:** Picking the right small cap stocks can grow your wealth over a period of time. Look for companies with generous free cash flows; carry less debt on their books; asset rich; profitable niche product or service and managers with large stakes in these companies.

**3:** Investing in small caps is riskier than investing in large caps. If you are able to take on additional levels of risk relative to large caps, dive in.

# 11- Stocks of Great Companies

## The Ten Lepers

### Luke 17:11-19

Now on his way to Jerusalem, Jesus traveled along the border between Samaria and Galilee. As he was going into a village, ten men who had leprosy met him. They stood at a distance and called out in a loud voice, "Jesus, Master, have pity on us!"

When he saw them, he said, "Go and meet the priests." And as they went, they were cleansed.

One of them, when he saw he was healed, came back, praising God in a loud voice. He threw himself at Jesus' feet and thanked him—and he was a Samaritan.

Jesus asked, "Were not all ten cleansed? Where are the other nine? Was no one found to return and give praise to God except this foreigner?"

Then he said to him, "Rise and go; your faith has made you well."

**Interpretation:**

It pays to have faith in the stock of a great company (see parable 10 for qualities of a great company).

Buy stocks of solid companies whenever their prices take a beating during panic selling or temporary setbacks. Buying a stock means being a part owner of the company whose stock you hold.

If you have done your research and figured out that a particular company is solid and has a great future, invest in it. Have faith. Buy these stocks and hold on to them for at least- five to ten years. You will be amply rewarded for your faith and patience.

**Bottom Line:**

The best investing approach is to choose great companies and stick with them for the long term.

# 12- Companies with Strong Foundations

## The Wise and Foolish Builders

### Matthew 7:24-29, Luke 6:46-49

Why do you call me, "Lord, Lord," and don't do what I say? If you listen and follow my teachings, then you are like the man who has built a house with a strong foundation. So, when natural calamities strike this house, it will be unaffected because it was well built.

But the one who hears my words and does not put them into practice is like a man who built a house without a foundation. During catastrophic events, the house will simply collapse and be destroyed.

**Interpretation:**

Companies with strong foundations can be found in every sector of the economy. Some of them are household names while others are not quite so well-known but are still leaders in their particular industries.

Check out companies that have been around for quite a while and have prospered in good markets and held their own when times were bad.

A market leader has often established products or services that have held off competitors and captured much of their market share. This is called the **economic moat**.

Google is an example of a company with a large economic moat. It's very difficult to compete with it in the search engine business. Google is forever innovating and coming out with new products. It is an immensely profitable company. Then, there's Coca Cola, Wal-Mart, McDonalds, ……….

Market leaders use their size to hold on to their competitive advantage. However, there are some past market leaders like IBM and General Motors who paused to hold their breath and are now just members of the pack.

Good companies usually pay dividends on a regular basis and have done so for many years.

Some of the key components of good companies are-

**1: Company History**- It is a solid company and has been around for quite a while and prospered in good markets and held its own when times were bad. It has efficient and solid management. Try a Google search of the key executives of your target company and check out their past records.

**2: Company Products or Services-** It has established products or services that have held off competitors and captured much of their market share. This is called the **economic moat.**

**3: Company's policies and operations-** The Company's management should be farsighted and adaptive without trying out unjustified investments and over-expansions.

**4: Earnings record-** The Company's earnings record should be stable and on an uptrend for the past five years.

**5: Return on Equity (ROE)-** A company cannot internally fund earnings growth faster than its ROE without raising additional cash by borrowing or selling mores shares. Look for companies whose five year ROE average is greater than 17%.

**6: Return on Capital (ROC)-** If a company carries no long term debt then its ROC equals ROE. If a company carries debt on its books then ROC will be greater than ROE. Look for companies whose five year ROC average is greater than 17%.

**7: Profit Margins-** Look for companies whose five year average pre-tax profit margins are equal or greater than 20% of industry average.

**8: Price / Cash flow ratio-** Look for companies whose price /cash flow ratio is less than 80% of the industry average and this ratio should be equal or greater than 0.1.

**9: Dividend History-** Good companies usually pay dividends on a regular basis and have done so for many years.

**10: Buyback of shares-** Good companies usually buy back their shares and reduce the outstanding shares in the market. A buyback generally increases shareholder value.

**Bottom Line:**

**1:** The above characteristics of good companies are not exhaustive but a starting point to do your research.

**2:** Large Institutional investors usually hold significant portions of these stocks in their portfolio and do not trade in them. Thus, there might not be major price rises in these stocks. These stocks will appreciate over time due to continued solid earnings and dividends.

**3:** Before you start investing in stocks or other financial investments, invest in a house. Your house should be the foundation or stepping stone to further success.

**4:** If you are going to invest in stocks, stay away from stocks of companies that do not have a strong foundation.

**5:** Buy stocks of great companies at attractive prices and hold on for the long term.

# 13- Brand Names

## Lamp on a Stand

### Matthew 5:14-15, Luke 8:16-18

You are the light of the world. A city on a hill cannot be hidden. Neither do people light a lamp and put it under a bowl. Instead they put it on its stand, and it gives light to everyone in the house. Whatever is hidden away will be brought out in the open, and whatever is covered up will be found out and exposed to the light. Therefore consider carefully how you listen. Whoever has something will be given more but whoever has nothing will have taken away from him even the little he thinks he has.

**Interpretation:**

What good is a product if potential buyers don't know about it? Companies need to market their products and announce its benefits to the whole world. If you want buyers then light a lamp!

If you are blessed with a particular talent, which the world needs to know, then advertise it. How would a potential employer know about it, if you keep quiet? If you have a book, product or a service to sell, let the whole world know about it. Advertise its benefits, if you want people to buy from you.

If you are investing in a stock then start with highly visible companies which has a large volume and is in trend. Make promising small caps a part of your portfolio, as well.

Great companies don't remain hidden for long. It's a matter of time before some astute investor or analyst tracks them down and exposes them to the world. Be alert.

**Bottom Line:**

Many great companies are brand names. Think Amazon, Google, Microsoft, WalMart, …..There are also thousands of smaller companies (small caps) that are not household names, but have the potential to turn into bright lamps (blue chips) tomorrow. Be alert and grab a piece of "soon to be discovered" promising companies. Your portfolio will shine with these stocks.

# 14- Shareholder Friendly Companies

## The Two Debtors

### Luke 7:36-50

One of the Pharisees named Simon invited Jesus to eat with him. Jesus accepted his invitation and went into the Pharisee's house and reclined at the table. And behold, a woman of the city, who was a sinner, when she learned that he was in the Pharisee's house, brought an alabaster flask of ointment, and stood behind him at his feet, weeping. She, then, began to wet his feet with her tears and wiped them with the hair of her head and kissed his feet and anointed them with the ointment.

Now when the Pharisee who had invited him saw this, he said to himself, "If this man was a prophet, he would have known who and what sort of woman this is who is touching him, for she is a sinner." And Jesus reading his thoughts said to him, "Simon, I have something to say to you."

Simon answered, "Say it, Teacher."

Jesus continued, "Two men owed money to a certain moneylender. One owed him five hundred coins, and the other fifty. Neither of them had the money to pay him back, so he canceled the debts of both. Now which of them will love him more?"

Simon replied, "I suppose the one who had the bigger debt canceled."

"You have judged correctly," Jesus said.

Then he turned toward the woman and said to Simon, "Do you see this woman? I came into your house. You did not give me any water for my feet, but she wet my feet with her tears and wiped them with her hair. You did not give me a kiss, but this woman, from the time I entered, has not stopped kissing my feet. You did not put oil on my head, but she has poured perfume on my feet.

Therefore, I tell you, her many sins have been forgiven—for she loved much. But he, who has been forgiven little, loves little."

**Interpretation and Bottom Line:**

Invest in stocks of shareholder friendly companies. These companies believe they will have loyal shareholders if the company treats them well. Grab shares of such companies because the management will treat you fairly and loyal shareholders will not sell their stocks in a hurry. There will be less price swings in such stocks.

# 15- Four Types of Companies

## Four Types of Soil

### Matthew 13:3-23

A farmer went out to sow seeds in his field. As he was scattering the seed, some fell along the path, and the birds came and ate it up. Some fell on rocky places, where it did not have much soil. It sprang up quickly, because the soil was shallow. But when the sun came up, the plants were scorched, and they withered because they had no root. Other seed fell among thorns, which grew up and choked the plants. Still other seed fell on good soil, where it produced a crop—a hundred, sixty or thirty times what was sown.

The disciples were confused and asked Jesus to explain the meaning of the above parable.

The Master replied, "Listen then to what the parable means:

**Seeds fallen on the path-** When anyone hears the divine message and does not understand it, the devil comes and snatches away what was sown in his heart. This is the seed sown along the path.

**Seeds fallen on rocky places-** The one who received the seed that fell on rocky places is the man who hears the word and at once receives it with joy.

But since he has no root, he lasts only a short time. When trouble or persecution comes because of the word, he quickly falls away.

**Seeds fallen over thorns-** The one who received the seed that fell among the thorns is the man who hears the word, but the worries of this life and the deceitfulness of wealth choke it, making it unfruitful.

**Seeds fallen on good soil-** The one who received the seed that fell on good soil is the man who hears the word and understands it. He produces a crop, yielding a hundred, sixty or thirty times what was sown."

**Interpretation:**

**Companies:** There are four types of companies-

**1: Companies fallen on the path-** The management of these companies is in a time warp and do not adapt to changes in the marketplace. They persist with obsolete technology, ancient management and marketing methods while the world around them is rapidly changing. They are soon overtaken by their companies and fall on the wayside. They become bankrupt; close down or are acquired by other companies.

**2: Companies fallen on rocky places-** The management of these companies are aware of the technological and production advances in their field but they are slow to adapt to changes for reasons best known to them.

**3: Companies fallen over thorns-** The management of these companies has great plans but is constrained by lack of finances and other factors. Think start-ups.

**4: Companies fallen on good soil-** These companies have everything going for them-good management, latest technology, strong balance sheet and market share. The stocks of these companies are the darlings of the stock market.

**Bottom Line:**

It pays to know which of the above four categories describe your company the best.

You will need to do a bit of homework before you figure out your company type and invest in its stock.

# 16- Stock Market Cycles

## Lazarus and the Rich Man

### Luke 16:19-31

There was a rich man who was dressed in purple and fine linen and lived in luxury every day. At his gate was laid a beggar named Lazarus, covered with sores and longing to eat what fell from the rich man's table. Even the dogs came and licked his sores. The time came when the beggar died and the angels carried him to Abraham's side.

The rich man also died and was buried. In hell, where he was in torment, he looked up and saw Abraham far away, with Lazarus by his side. So he called to him, "Father Abraham, have pity on me and send Lazarus to dip the tip of his finger in water and cool my tongue, because I am in agony in this fire."

But Abraham replied, "Son, remember that in your lifetime you received your good things, while Lazarus received bad things, but now he is comforted here and you are in agony. And besides all this, between us and you a great chasm has been fixed, so that those who want to go from here to you cannot, nor can anyone cross over from there to us."

He answered, "Then I beg you, father, send Lazarus to my father's house, for I have five brothers. Let him warn them, so that they will not also come to this place of torment."

Abraham replied, "They have Moses and the Prophets. Let them listen to them."

"No, Father Abraham," he said, "but if someone from the dead goes to them, they will repent."

He said to him, "If they do not listen to Moses and the Prophets, they will not be convinced even if someone rises from the dead.''

**Interpretation:**

What did you figure out from the above parable?

Cycles rule every aspect of our life. Take humans or other living beings. We pass through many cycles: birth-childhood- adult stage- old age- death. Then there are other cycles like rags to riches, obscurity to fame and so on. In the above parable, the rich man had everything going for him on earth and then after death, hell. On the other hand, Lazarus who was a beggar on earth enjoyed the luxuries of heaven after death.

The stock market also runs on cycles.

There are four phases of a market cycle-

**1: Rising phase-** This period occurs when the bearish period is nearing its end and wise investors start buying, figuring the worst is behind them. Most of the pessimists or panic sellers have sold their holdings which are available for grabs at very attractive prices.

**2: Bullish phase-** The market is in a bullish phase. Buyers ruled by greed are jumping on the bandwagon and buying stocks at higher and higher prices. During this time, wise investors who had bought stocks during the Rising phase at low prices start selling to gullible investors. After a while, the prices become unsustainable and soon start falling.

**3: Bearish phase-** This is the beginning of the bearish phase. Sellers have started offloading their positions. Prices are going down. Many investors are selling at a loss.

**4: Bottom phase-** All hopes of recovery are belied at this stage. The remaining sellers sell their stocks at huge losses. Value investors step in to buy these shares at bargain prices.

**Bottom Line:**

**1:** The stock market like everything else runs on cycles. What goes up (bullish trend) has to come down (bearish trend) after a while.

**2:** After every bull there is a bear and after every bear there is a bull. After every correction there is a recovery.

**3:** During bullish periods, investors are so greed driven that they will not listen to even God if He told them not to buy at such unrealistic prices.

**4:** The same sentiment goes for bearish periods. Most investors will hesitate to buy when the prices have almost touched the bottom. Wise investors consider this as a buy signal and start fishing for great bargains.

**5:** Buy stocks during bearish periods and sell during a bull market.

**6: Technical Analysis** is the way to go for understanding the stock market cycles. Reading the stock and market charts will help you understand the price action of a stock. Read good books on this subject. Millions of investors and traders swear by Technical Analysis so there's something in it.

**7:** Finally, listen to Warren Buffett's sage advice- 'I will tell you how to become rich. Be fearful when others are greedy. Be greedy when others are fearful.'

# 17- The Stock Market Is Unpredictable

## The Weather Signs

### Luke 12:54-59, Matthew 26:2, Mark 8:11-13

When you see a cloud rising in the west, you say at once, "A shower is coming" and so it happens. And when you see the south wind blowing, you say, "There will be scorching heat" and it happens. You hypocrites! You know how to interpret the appearance of earth and sky, but why do you not know how to interpret the present time? And why do you not judge for yourselves what is right? As you go with your accuser before the magistrate, make an effort to settle with him on the way, lest he drag you to the judge and the judge hands you over to the officer, and the officer puts you in prison. I tell you, you will never get out till you have paid the very last copper.

**Interpretation:**

The stock market is unpredictable and uncontrollable. Market gurus and experts go to great lengths to predict the stock market. Some of them are successful for a limited period of time before Mr. Market brings them to their knees.

Investors must refrain from acting upon stock market predictions. In the above parable, Jesus inquires, "You know how to interpret the appearance of earth and sky, but why do you not know how to interpret the present time?"

It's the same with the market. It's easier to predict long term trends than very short term trends. Many day traders have lost their shirts trying to predict the same day direction (present time) of a stock or the market. If you made a wrong investing decision then get out of this position before you are down to your very last "copper."

**Bottom Line:**

**1:** Analysts and other stock market gurus have a hard time predicting the future of a single company let alone a market made up of thousands of companies.

**2:** Long term trends are a bit easier to predict than short term trends.

**3:** If you have made a wrong investing decision then get out of this position before you are down to your very last "copper."

# 18- Sell I

## The Sheep and the Goats

### Matthew 25:31-46

When the Son of Man comes in his glory, and all the angels with him, he will sit on his throne in heavenly glory. All the nations will be gathered before him, and he will separate the people one from another as a shepherd separates the sheep from the goats. He will put the sheep on his right and the goats on his left.

Then the King will say to those on his right, "Come, you who are blessed by my Father, take your inheritance, the kingdom prepared for you since the creation of the world. For I was hungry and you gave me something to eat; I was thirsty and you gave me something to drink; I was a stranger and you invited me in; I needed clothes and you clothed me; I was sick and you looked after me; I was in prison and you came to visit me."

Then the righteous will answer him, "Lord, when did we see you hungry and feed you, or thirsty and give you something to drink? When did we see you a stranger and invite you in or needing clothes and clothe you? When did we see you sick, visit you in prison or come to visit you?"

The King will reply, "I tell you the truth, whatever you did for one of the least of these brothers of mine, you did for me."

Then he will say to those on his left, "Depart from me, you who are cursed, into the eternal fire prepared for the devil and his angels. For I was hungry and you gave me nothing to eat; I was thirsty and you gave me nothing to drink; I was a stranger and you did not invite me in; I needed clothes and you did not clothe me; I was sick and in prison and you did not look after me."

They also will answer, "Lord, when did we see you hungry or thirsty or a stranger or needing clothes or sick or in prison, and did not help you?"

He will reply, "I tell you the truth, whatever you did not do for one of the least of these, you did not do for me."

Then they will go away to eternal punishment, but the righteous to eternal life!

**Interpretation and Bottom Line:**
If an investment or a stock has not achieved your investment objectives, sell them quickly. They are doing your portfolio no good.

# 19- Sell II

## The Barren Fig Tree

### Luke 13:6-9

A man planted a fig tree in his vineyard and checked on the tree frequently to see if it bore any fruit, but he was always disappointed.

Finally, he said to his gardener, "For three years now I've been coming to look for fruit on this fig tree and haven't found any. Cut it down! Why should it use up the soil?"

"Sir, give it one more chance. Leave it another year, and I will give it special attention and plenty of fertilizer. If we get figs next year, fine. If not, then you can cut it down," the gardener replied.

**Interpretation:**

Are you holding on to stocks that have underperformed even after holding on to them for years? Are you suffering from loss aversion bias? Don't you think you should sell off these investments and invest in something more profitable?

Many investors make the mistake of holding on to stocks which have not shown any returns for ages. They reckon these stocks will someday appreciate and vindicate their foolish buying decision. Figured out the cost of holding on to such dead investments? Is it worthwhile to hold on to such stocks or sell them off?

**Bottom Line:**

Can you guarantee that a stock will ever come back?

No! If you are patiently waiting for the stock to break even - the point at which profit equals losses – it will never come. You can seriously erode your returns. Sell before further losses occur.

# 20- Exit a Losing Trade

## The Two Sons

### Matthew 21:28-32

A man had two sons. He went to the first and said, "Son, go and work today in the vineyard." "I will not," he answered, but later he changed his mind and went. And he went to the other son and said the same. The son answered in the affirmative but he did not go.

"Which of the two did what his father wanted?" Jesus questioned.

"The first," they answered.

Jesus said to them, "I tell you the truth, the tax collectors and the prostitutes are entering the kingdom of God ahead of you. For John came to you to show you the way of righteousness, and you did not believe him, but the tax collectors and the prostitutes did. And even after you saw this, you did not afterward change your minds and believe him."

**Interpretation:**

Here Jesus talks about not being rigid with one's initial decision and sticking to it. Does your pride prevent you from listening to your inner voice?

Check out the following situation-

You make a decision to buy a stock and shortly after calling your broker, you realize your reason for making the trade was completely off track. Instead of admitting your mistake and getting out for a small loss, you stay in the position. Inevitably, what happens? Your small loss turns into a very big one.

**Bottom Line:**

If you have made a mistake, accept it and get out of a losing position quickly. You might suffer a huge loss, if you don't.

# 21- Averaging Down and Derivatives

## The Evil Tenants of the Vineyard

### Matthew 21:33-44

There was a landowner who planted a vineyard. He put a wall around it, dug a winepress in it and built a watchtower. Then he rented the vineyard to some farmers and went away on a journey.

When the harvest time approached, he sent his servants to the tenants to collect his fruit. The tenants seized his servants; they beat one, killed another, and stoned a third. Then he sent other servants to them, more than the first time, and the tenants treated them the same way.

Last of all, he sent his son to them. "They will respect my son," he said. But when the tenants saw the son, they said to each other, "This is the owner's son. Let's kill him." So they took him and threw him out of the vineyard and killed him. Therefore, when the owner of the vineyard comes, what will he do to those tenants?

"He will bring those wretches to a wretched end," they replied, "and he will rent the vineyard to other tenants, who will give him his share of the crop at harvest time."

Jesus continued, "Have you never read in the Scriptures-The stone the builders rejected has become the capstone; the Lord has done this, and isn't it awesome? Therefore, I tell you that the kingdom of God will be taken away from you and given to the people who will produce its fruit. He who falls on this stone will be broken to pieces, but he on whom it falls will be crushed."

**Interpretation:**

The **'Averaging Down'** strategy and **'Derivatives'** are like the tenants of the vineyard. You could lose a lot if you make a wrong move with these strategies.

Remember the parable 11- **'Old Cloth and New Wine / Wineskins'** where you were warned patching your losses with more cash infusion could be a costly mistake? 'Averaging Down' strategy will not work if the share price continues to nosedive.

Stay off derivatives if you don't understand them. They are like the tenants of the vineyard. Derivatives' trading is a zero sum game. It will eat up your entire investment and more if you are wrong.

You will be like the landowner in the above parable- all your servants (margin money) and your son (capital) will be killed (lose everything).

# 22- Adapt or Perish

## Old Cloth and New Wine / Wineskins

### Matthew 9:16-17

No one sews a piece of unshrunked cloth on an old garment; for the patch pulls away from the garment, and the tear is made worse.

Nor do they put new wine into old wineskins, or else the wineskins break, the wine is spilled, and the wineskins are ruined.

But they put new wine into new wineskins, and both are preserved.

**Interpretation:**

Jesus was right. If you stick with old systems, ideas or manufacturing processes and fail to anticipate the future, you are going the way of the dinosaurs. Patchwork won't do. Adapt or perish.

If you look back 25 years, you will find many of the then world's top companies are no longer at the top, today. They have shrunk, grown obsolete or acquired by nimble competitors. Remember Digital Equipment, Polaroid, Wang laboratories?

Automobile giants like General Motors and Ford did not foresee the demand for small, fuel efficient cars which the Japanese companies unleashed in the US. They continued to make large, gas guzzling cars at a time when oil prices were spiraling up. They woke up late to realize their follies and losing their market leader status.

GM is now consumed by the nightmarish safety crisis, announcing the recall of 8.4 million more vehicles worldwide — most of them for an ignition defect similar to the flaw that the company failed to disclose in other models for more than a decade. It's going to cost billions in lawsuits. Ford under Alan Mulally (now retired) is on higher ground. It's doing great for now.

Does Eastman Kodak ring a bell? It was one of the most successful companies unto the 1990's. It continued with its old film and camera making business when the whole world had taken to digital photography and smart phones that doubled as cameras. Kodak missed out on all this. In January 2012, Kodak filed for Chapter 11 bankruptcy protection. On September 3, 2013, Kodak emerged from bankruptcy having shed its large legacy liabilities and exited several businesses. On March 12, 2014, Kodak announced that the Board of Directors had elected Jeffrey J. Clarke as CEO.

Kodak has shed its old clothes. Let's wait and watch.

The bottom line is if a company fails to notice something new in the marketplace and continue with their old business, which is on the way to obsolescence, then they will have a tough time coming out of the woods.

Before you invest in a company's stock, check whether the company's business plans are sustainable for the next five years. Check out its business history. Has it rapidly adapted to changes in the market place? Who runs the company? An aging founder who still lives in the past or is it some innovative guy with a great reputation behind him? You can Google the names of the key executives to find out who they are and what their track record is. Do your homework.

Suppose you have just bought a stock on a personal hunch or tip. You have no idea what the company does. You are in it for the short term. After taking a position, the stock starts falling. Hey! What now?

How will you ascertain if this price drop is temporary or a reaction to something more serious? Are you going to buy more shares to bring down the average cost of your investment? What if the stock continues its dizzying fall? What is going to happen to your **'Averaging Down'** strategy? This Averaging Down strategy is nothing but patching up an old garment with an 'unshrunked' cloth which continues to tear the garment.

Jesus has warned us about this.

So, your best bet when investing in a stock would be to have a stop loss of 5% below your purchase price. If your share starts falling you will be out of your position with a small loss.

**Bottom Line:**

**1:** Whether you are a company or an individual investor, you need to adapt to the changing scenario or wither.

**2:** Be nimble enough to get out of a losing position quickly. Don't try to patch up your mistakes with more cash infusion. It can be a costly mistake. **'Averaging Down'** strategy will not work if the share price continues to nosedive.

**3:** If an investment technique or business process doesn't work, try out something new instead of tinkering with the old method.

# 23- Be On Guard

## Watchfulness

### Mark 13:32-37, Luke 12:35-40

Be on guard! Be alert! You do not know when that time will come. It's like a man going away. He leaves his house and puts his servants in charge, each with his assigned task, and tells the one at the door to keep watch, so that when he comes and knocks they can immediately open the door for him. It will be good for those servants whose master finds them ready, even if he comes very late in the night. But remember this- If the master had known at what hour the thief was coming, he would not have let his house be broken into. You also must be ready, because the Son of Man will come at an hour when you do not expect him.

**Interpretation:**

Does the above warning not ring true for the stock markets? Watchfulness is the key to playing safe in the market.

The stock market's a rocky place to be. Anything can happen at any time. A small rumor, a trading glitch, Fed rate cuts or a war can bring down the market.

You need to watch out for sudden market changes or price actions, every day. Is the trend right? You need to be alert to take appropriate decisions if something goes wrong. Watch out for price swings or sudden free-falls of your stock's price. Is it a temporary fear factor? Are the company's fortunes in a downswing? Is it serious? Are the interest rates going to change? Is the country going to be affected by wars, terrorist attacks, economic slowdown and other factors?

Are there any unexplained changes in your personal portfolio? If so, investigate and take immediate action to set them right. Change your passwords often. Watch out for internet scam artists.

Having stop loss orders will limit your losses if there's a downslide.

Keep a tight control over your debt and personal finances.

Check out the conditions before you take buy or sell decisions.

**Bottom Line:**

Be vigilant and informed about your portfolio; your debt and finances; the financial markets, and the general economy to help you face the unforeseen surprises or shocks which the market will throw on your lap.

# 24- Be Alert

## Signs from a Fig Tree

### Matthew 24:32-44

Now learn this lesson from the fig tree: As soon as its twigs get tender and its leaves come out, you know that summer is near. Even so, when you see all these things, you know that it is near, right at the door. Believe me; this generation will certainly not pass away until all these things have happened. Heaven and earth will pass away, but my words will never pass away. No one knows about that day or hour, not even the angels in heaven, nor the Son, but only the Father.

As it was in the days of Noah, so it will be at the coming of the Son of Man. For in the days before the flood, people were eating and drinking, marrying and giving in marriage, up to the day Noah entered the ark and they knew nothing about what would happen until the flood came and took them all away. That is how it will be at the coming of the Son of Man.

Two men will be in the field; one will be taken and the other left. Two women will be grinding with a hand mill; one will be taken and the other left. Therefore keep watch, because you do not know on what day your Lord will come.

But understand this: If the owner of the house had known at what time of night the thief was coming, he would have kept watch and would not have let his house be broken into. So you also must be ready, because the Son of Man will come at an hour when you do not expect him.

**Interpretation:**

In the above parable, Jesus speaks about uncertainties in our life. We'll never be able to guess when the current situation will change and affect our lives. So, we need to be vigilant and not be caught on the wrong foot.

Pay attention to what's happening with your investments. No stock is safe forever. If there is some distressing news in the company or the economy, stocks take a dive. Even the bluest blue chip can turn into a dud chip. We should not close our eyes and enjoy the sun even when the stock market's rocking. Cycles rule the markets. The positive trend can change anytime and before we open our eyes our investments will have red ink over them.

So, stay awake always.

**Bottom Line:**

Be alert. Keep a watch over stock market trends, global news, adverse company and economic news. If there is a sudden reversal you will be in a position to take immediate corrective action.

# 25- Don't Be Overconfident

## Master and Servant

### Luke 17:7-10

Suppose one of you had a servant plowing or looking after the sheep. When the servant comes in from working in the field, would you say, "Come in and sit down to eat?"

Would you not rather say, "Prepare my supper, get yourself ready and wait on me while I eat and drink and after that you may eat and drink?"

Would you thank the servant because he did what he was told to do? It's the same with you. When you have done everything you are told to do, you should say that you are unworthy servants and have only done the work you should do.'

**Interpretation:**

Don't be overconfident with your stock picking abilities. If your trade was successful be humble. Remember the stock market is the master and you are the servant. The master can always teach the servant a lesson. The next trade could bring you down to your knees.

**Bottom Line:**

Humility, patience and discipline are the hallmarks of a wise and successful investor.

# 26- Don't Be Reckless

## The Rich Fool

### Luke 12:15-21

Jesus cautioned, "Watch out! Be on your guard against all kinds of greed; a man's life does not consist in the abundance of his possessions."

And, then, he told them this parable:

The ground of a certain rich man produced a good crop.

He thought to himself, "What shall I do? I have no place to store my crops." Then he said, "This is what I will do. I will tear down my barns and build bigger ones, and there I will store all the grain and goods for personal use. I will have plenty of good things laid up for many years. Yeah! I will take life easy- eat, drink and be merry."

But God said to him, "You fool! This very night your life will be demanded from you. Then who will get what you have prepared for yourself?"

This is how it will be with anyone who stores up things for himself but is not rich toward God.

Jesus continued, "Take no thought for your life, what you shall eat; neither for the body, what you shall put on. The life is more than meat, and the body is more than raiment. Consider the ravens: for they neither sow nor reap; which neither have storehouse nor barn; and God feeds them: how much more are you better than the fowls?

And which of you with taking thought can add to his stature one cubit?

If you are not able to do that thing which is least, why take which was intended for the rest?

Consider the lilies how they grow: they toil not, they spin not; and yet I say unto you, that Solomon in all his glory was not arrayed like one of these.

If then God so clothe the grass, which is to day in the field, and tomorrow is cast into the oven; how much more will he clothe you, O ye of little faith?

And seek not ye what ye shall eat, or what ye shall drink, neither be ye of doubtful mind.

For all these things do the nations of the world seek after: and your Father knoweth that ye have need of these things? But rather seek ye the kingdom of God; and all these things shall be added unto you.

Fear not, little flock; for it is your Father's good pleasure to give you the kingdom. Sell that you have, and give alms; provide yourselves bags which wax not old, a treasure in the heavens that faileth not, where no thief approacheth, neither moth corrupteth."

**Interpretation:**

Some companies go about expanding too quickly or acquiring new businesses after sales are going well. They do this by dipping into the company funds or by borrowings.

Will the market support the expansion or will there be no increase in sales after expansion?

What if there's a sudden downtrend?

Was the price paid for acquiring a new company too high?

How has the market taken to the stock of such companies?

Invest in companies that promote environmental stewardship, human rights, consumer protection' alternate energy / clean technology efforts and philanthropic activities.

**Bottom Line:**

**1:** If you are buying into a stock of a particular company, check out whether the company is trying to expand its business. It's better to wait and watch whether the expansion plans work out, before you invest in this company. It's always safer to buy stocks of companies which are fiscally prudent and can maintain a consistent level of debt and easily cover interest costs.

**2: Philanthropic Investing:** This is a style of investing where the investor has a clear philanthropic goal and a strategy to achieve that goal. A philanthropic investor funds a project where he can expect a traditional financial return as well as societal benefits.

**3: Socially Responsible Investing:** A socially responsible investor avoids companies involved in alcohol, tobacco, gambling, weapons, gambling, contraception related activities. More and more people are into Socially Responsible Investing.

**4: Practice philanthropy:** It feels good to give back to the society that made you rich. Support the poor, the underprivileged or a worthy cause. Blessings will be your returns from this investment.

# 27- Control Your Emotions

## The Great Banquet

### Matthew 22:1-14, Luke 14:15-24

A certain man was preparing a great banquet and invited many guests. He sent his servants to those who had been invited to the banquet to tell them to come, but they refused to come.

The first said, "I have just bought a field, and I must go and see it. Please excuse me."

Another said, "I have just bought five yoke of oxen, and I am on my way to try them out. Please excuse me."

Still another said, "I just got married, so I can't come."

The servant came back and reported this to his master. Then the owner of the house became angry and ordered his servant, "Go out quickly into the streets and alleys of the town and bring in the poor, the crippled, the blind and the lame."

The servant replied, "Sir, what you ordered has been done, but there is still room."

"Go out to the roads and country lanes and make them come in, so that my house will be full. I tell you, not one of those men who were invited will get a taste of my banquet," ordered the master.

**Interpretation:**

The guy in the above parable was not thinking straight. Do you think he would enjoy the banquet with just anybody? Wasn't he throwing good money after the bad and the useless? Why did he not cancel the banquet and wait another day?

The same rule applies to your investing methodology. Don't let emotions guide your investment decisions. Don't throw your money into the market blindly. Avoid self-destructive behavior. The market is not a tranquilizer. Do something else.

You don't need to trade every day. It could be a lousy trading day when nothing seems to go right. If you have placed a limit buy order for some 'must have' stocks and your order doesn't get executed, don't lose your marbles.

Take a deep breath and tell yourself to stop! Don't behave like the guy in the above parable. Keep your ego in check. Don't try to buy any other stock on a whim because you need to. There's no compulsion that you need to buy or sell a stock if some of your earlier orders don't get executed. You might end up buying a lousy stock or selling a great stock from your portfolio.

The parable is a warning signal for traders who after making one wrong call keep on trading across the field to recoup their initial loss. This usually results in more losses which can spiral out of control.

Resist this tendency and switch off your cell phone or trading monitor. Wait for the dust to settle. There's always another day.

**Bottom Line:**

**1:** Patience, humility and discipline are the hallmarks of a great investor.

**2:** If your trades could not be executed then stay put. Don't let such incidents piss you off. Think straight. Otherwise, you might end up buying a lousy stock or selling a great stock from your portfolio.

**3:** If you are a trader and if your position goes against you, liquidate it immediately. Don't try to cover your losses by executing more trades. If your day's not good, you will end up with huge losses.

**4:** If you don't get the right people to your banquet then just don't invite anybody else. These guys will only waste your money and nothing else. The same goes for investing. If you don't get the right stock then don't go for less worthy stocks.

# 28- Don't Panic!

## The Weeds

### Matthew 13:24-30, 36-43

The kingdom of heaven is like a man who sowed good seed in his field. At night, while everyone was sleeping, his enemy came and sowed weeds among the wheat, and went away. When the wheat sprouted and formed heads, the weeds also appeared.

The farmhands came to him and said, "Sir, didn't you sow good seed in your field? Where then did the weeds come from?"

"An enemy did this," he replied.

The farmhands asked him, "Do you want us to go and pull them up?"

"No," he answered, "because while you are pulling the weeds, you might pull out the wheat with them. Let them both grow together until the harvest. At that time I will tell the harvesters. First collect the weeds and tie them in bundles to be burned; then gather the wheat and bring it into my barn."

The disciples requested Jesus to explain the significance of this parable.

He answered, "The one who sowed the good seed is the Son of Man. The field is the world, and the good seed stands for the sons of the kingdom. The weeds are the sons of the devil, and the enemy who sows them is the devil himself! The harvest is the end of the age, and the harvesters are angels.

As the weeds are pulled up and burned in the fire, so it will be at the end of the age. The Son of Man will send out his angels, and they will weed out of his kingdom everything that causes sin and all who do evil. They will throw them into the fiery furnace, where there will be weeping and gnashing of teeth. Then the righteous will shine like the sun in the kingdom of their Father.

**Interpretation:**

If there's a sudden and unexpected panic selling situation don't join the herd. Figure out the cause of this panic selling. Is it justified? Don't try selling your stocks during this period. You will end up selling your good stocks at a huge loss. Bad stocks will find no takers. Instead treat this panic selling situation as a perfect situation for great buying opportunities.

**Bottom Line:**

**1:** Don't panic. Most people go over the edge and sell their profitable shares in panic situations. It's a perfect situation for great buying opportunities.

**2:** Listen to Warren Buffett's sage advice- 'I will tell you how to become rich. Be fearful when others are greedy. Be greedy when others are fearful.'

**3:** Peter Lynch once said that he was the best stock picker on Wall Street for 13 years because he pulled up the weeds and watered the flowers.

# 29- Check on Your Investments

## The Fishing Net

### Matthew 13:47-50

Once again, the kingdom of heaven is like a net that was let down into the lake and caught all kinds of fish. When it was full, men pulled it ashore and sat down and sorted the good into containers but threw away the bad. This is how it will be at the end of the age. The angels will come and separate the wicked from the righteous and throw them into the fiery furnace, where there will be weeping and gnashing of teeth.

**Interpretation:**

Every investor needs to periodically check his investments. If a particular stock or any other investment is an underperformer, he should sell them off quickly. The cost of waiting for a particular investment to break even is too high.

Your fishing net (diversified portfolio) should have a good mix of stocks, bonds and other investments. Diversifying your portfolio helps mitigate your risk. If one class of investment fares badly, another class performs nicely. If your portfolio comprises of only stocks then it's best to hold stocks from several different industries. That way, if one area of the economy goes into the dumps, you have something to fall back on.

**Bottom Line:**

Keep the performers and sell the non-performers from your portfolio.

# 30- Missing Stocks and Money

## The Lost Sheep, Lost Coin

### Matthew 18:12-14, Luke 15:8-10

Suppose one of you had a hundred sheep and lost one. Wouldn't you leave the ninety-nine in the wilderness and go after the lost one until you found it? When found, you can be sure you would put it across your shoulders, rejoicing, and when you got home call in your friends and neighbors, saying, "Celebrate with me! I've found my lost sheep!"

In the same way your Father in heaven is not willing that any of these little ones should be lost.

Or suppose a woman has ten silver coins and loses one. Does she not light a lamp, sweep the house and search carefully until she finds it? And when she finds it, she calls her friends and neighbors together and says, "Rejoice with me! I have found my lost coin!"

In the same way, I tell you, there is rejoicing in the presence of the angels of God over one sinner who repents.'

**Interpretation:**

Wouldn't you like to track down your missing stocks and money owed to you? Wouldn't you rejoice after you receive the missing windfall?

**1: Unclaimed money-** You may have unclaimed funds in old bank accounts, insurance policies, utility deposits, dividend payments, escrow accounts, or because of wages owed to you by a former employer. This site **http://www.missingmoney.com/** provides a way to search for all types of missing money at once. This is a free site. When you first search, you are prompted to enter your home state. There are some states which have not participated in this site and if the company whose stock you are trying to track down was in one of these states, You will need to go on to the free website at **www.unclaimed.org** set up by **The National Association of Unclaimed Property Administrators (NAUPA)** that will link you to the appropriate department in each state that holds unclaimed funds.

**2: Missing stocks-** If you are locating your missing stocks in a company that has changed its name or bought over by another company with a new name, then you need to remember this- if shares still have value and go unclaimed, the company is supposed to submit those to the states for safekeeping. The account will be in the name of the stockholder, not the company. The shares will either be held by the state where the stockholder lived when they bought the stock or in the state where the company is based or in the state in which it is incorporated.

**3: Income tax refund checks-** This site **http://bit.ly/1mZBhbf** sponsored by the **National Taxpayers Union**, will help you track down any lost tax refunds or unclaimed money owed to you by the IRS.

**4: Old pension Plan-** This site **http://1.usa.gov/1yzjlZe** is where to start your search for old pension plans that failed.

**5: Unclaimed Retirement Benefits-** This site **https://www.unclaimedretirementbenefits.com/** is useful for tracking your balance in an old employer retirement plan. It can also be useful for executors of estates who are trying to track down unclaimed money on behalf of a loved one or deceased.

**6: Unclaimed Treasury Bonds-** This site **http://1.usa.gov/1kB7YrA** will help to check out if your bonds are still paying interest and search for any other unclaimed sources of money from the Treasury.

**7: Unclaimed Life Insurance Benefits-** This site **http://www.demutualization-claims.com/** is the place to start your search for your unclaimed Life insurance benefits.

**Bottom Line:**

Want to locate your missing "sheep" or "coin?" Try the above sites. Rejoice!

# 31- Track Your Expenses

## The Cost of Being a Disciple

### Luke 14:25-35

Suppose one of you wants to build a tower. Won't you first sit down and estimate the cost to see if you have enough money to complete it?

For if you lay the foundation and are not able to finish it, everyone who sees it will ridicule you, saying that you could not complete what you began.

Or suppose a king is about to go to war against another king. Won't he first sit down and consider whether he is able, with ten thousand men, to oppose the one coming against him with twenty thousand?

If he is not able, he will send a delegation while the other is still a long way off and will ask for terms of peace.

In the same way, any of you who do not give up everything he has cannot be my disciple. Salt is good, but if it loses its saltiness, how can it be made salty again? It is fit neither for the soil nor for the manure pile; No, it is thrown out.

**Interpretation:**

Pay attention: Jesus advises us to check out our resources before taking on any project. If the resources are not enough, then one should not go ahead with the plans.

The above parable is applicable for companies that use leverage to borrow more than they can afford, gearing up balance sheets in an attempt to try and increase business performance. If their business plans succeed, this strategy can work well. If the strategy goes terribly wrong then you have companies that borrowed too much, increased their leverage to unsustainable levels, income not enough to cover debt costs leading to restructuring or defaults. Companies need to display that they are fiscally prudent and can maintain a consistent level of debt and easily cover interest costs over a period of several years.

Then there are the investors and speculators who bet more than they could afford on the housing bubble back in 2008.

Never invest any money that you cannot safely afford to lose. Learn to be fiscally prudent.

Before you start investing in stocks, check out whether you have a secure job or business and an emergency fund of six to twelve months of living expenses in a savings account. This money should not be used for investing. This is your safety parachute if things go wrong.

You should have a separate investment account. You must allocate 10% to 25% of your after-tax income to this account every year. Ideally you should have $ 10,000 in your investment account and be prepared to lose it all. It's not necessary to start big in the stock market. Remember Jesus' warning and invest within your means. If your investment nest-egg to start with is smaller then start small.

You can start with as little as $20 to invest in **Dividend Reinvestment Plans (DRPs)** or **Drips** and **Direct Stock Purchase Plans (DSPs)** which allow you to buy a stock directly from the companies or their agents. The real benefit of these plans is that you aren't paying a hefty commission to a broker and the fees charged by the companies are very minimal.

One drawback is that not every company offers these plans so you may be somewhat limited in your selection.

If you are starting out with a small amount to invest and want to make frequent purchases (dollar-cost averaging) then these plans are for you. Once you are in the plan, you can set up an automatic payment plan, and you are allowed to purchase fractions of shares.

If you have a few hundred dollars or a grand to start with, then you can buy an index fund or some low cost mutual funds.

You should also seriously consider opening a **discount brokerage account**. Focus on accounts that require a zero or minimum initial deposit. You can now start researching and perhaps buying a few stocks. Try to keep your brokerage fees and other investing costs) to less than 2% of the transaction value.

If your brokerage account has a margin account- before using it remember what Jesus said in the above parable. Margin accounts let you purchase stocks with borrowed money. They can increase your returns if your stock calls are right but they'll also increase your risk. You will have to pay all that margin money back at some point along with interest – don't you forget that. Remember this- your broker has total control over the collateral for the loan and can force you to sell stock if it thinks you are going to default on its loan.

**Bottom Line:**

**1:** Invest within your means. Don't bite more than you can swallow!

**2:** Learn to control your expenses. You should know exactly how much you invested in a stock and what returns you received from it.

**3:** If you have a small sum to start with, invest in DRPs and DSPs.

**4:** Don't invest using margin money. You could lose a lot of money if your position turns against you.

**5:** Stay away from futures and commodities trading if you are a novice.

# 32- Do Your Taxes I

## The Pharisee and the Tax Collector

### Luke 18:9-14

Two men went up to the temple to pray, one a Pharisee and the other a tax collector. The Pharisee stood up and prayed about himself, "God, I thank you that I am not like other men—robbers, evildoers, adulterers—or even like this tax collector. I fast twice a week and give a tenth of all I get."

But the tax collector stood at a distance. He would not even look up to heaven, but beat his breast and said, "God, have mercy on me, a sinner."

Thus, the tax collector went home justified before God. He who humbles himself will be exalted and he who exalts himself will be humbled.

**Interpretation:**

Never ever think you can outsmart the Market or the IRS. Be modest. Don't be over confident while investing. The stock market can be a very humbling place. No one can consistently beat the market. The market is always right. Remember this and stay humble.

Do your taxes or the "sinful" tax collector will come knocking at your door.

**Bottom Line:**

**1:** It's not possible to consistently beat the market. If a position turns against you, do not lament that you were correct and the market wrong.

No one's going to hear you. You will suffer a loss if you do not close your losing position quickly and limit your loss.

**2:** Always, use a stop loss to limit your losses.

**3:** Don't cheat on your taxes or the tax collector will punish you for your "sins."

# 33- Do Your Taxes II

## The Doctor and the Sick

### Luke 5:27-32, Matthew 9:12, Mark 2:17

After this he went out, and saw a tax collector, named Levi, sitting at the tax office; and he said to him, "Follow me." And he left everything, and rose and followed him. And Levi made him a great feast in his house; and there was a large company of tax collectors and others sitting at table with them. And the Pharisees and their scribes murmured against his disciples, saying, "Why do you eat and drink with tax collectors and sinners?" And Jesus answered them, "Those who are well have no need of a physician, but those who are sick. I have not come to call the righteous, but sinners to repentance."

**Interpretation:**

Tax collectors seem to be a despised lot since ancient times. Don't we curse the IRS when the tax season draws near? There's an old saying, "In life, two things are inevitable: Death & Taxes." It's impossible to avoid either but we can try to minimize the taxman's impact over our investments. Talk to your "doctor" (tax planner).

Let's not curse the sinner (IRS) and instead figure out *how to avoid paying tax legally*.

Here's how-

**1: Subtracting Capital Gains from Capital Losses within the Same Year-** Capital losses can be used against capital gains, and short-term losses can be deducted from short-term gains, significantly reducing your tax burden.

**2: Broker Fees-** Don't forget to add the transferring fees and brokerage to the amount you paid for a stock when determining your cost basis. When you sell the shares, subtract the commission from the sale price of the stocks. Think of these costs as a write-off because they are direct expenses incurred when you invested.

**3: Long Term Capital Gains-** It can prove very beneficial to hold onto your stocks for at least one year. Short-term capital gains (less than one year) are always taxed at a higher rate than long-term ones (more than one year).

**4: Dividends-** Are you aware that you can reduce your taxable gain if dividends are automatically reinvested in your mutual fund? Reinvested dividends increase your investment in a fund and thus reduce your taxable gain or increase your capital loss. Keep accurate records of the reinvested dividends and take advantage of this rule during the tax season.

**5: Bonds-** If you bought bonds, remember to report the interest income on your tax return. Are you aware that if you bought the bond in between interest payments (most bonds pay interest every six months), you may not have to pay tax on interest accrued prior to your purchase? You will need to report the entire interest amount you received, but you will be able to subtract the accrued amount on a separate line. Most municipal bonds are issued with tax-exempt status- the returns they generate do not need to be claimed when you file your tax return.

**6: Tax-Deferred Programs-** If you make your purchases through a tax deferred account, **Individual Retirement Account (IRA)** and **Simplified Employment Pension (SEP)**, you are not taxed on the funds until you withdraw, at which point you are taxed at the rate of your income tax bracket.

**Bottom Line:**

**1:** We hate doing taxes, but there's no escape hatch!

**2:** The tax guys (IRS) are neither sinners nor bullies. They're doing their job. Taxes run the economy. We need to pay our taxes.

**3:** It is impossible to avoid either death or taxes but we can try to minimize our tax burden.

# 34-Rumors and Tips

## What Defiles a Person?

### Matthew 15:10-20

And Jesus called the people to him and said to them, "Hear and understand: it is not what goes into the mouth that defiles a person, but what comes out of the mouth- this defiles a person."

Then the disciples came and said to him, "Do you know that the Pharisees were offended when they heard this saying?"

He answered, "Every plant that my heavenly Father has not planted will be rooted up. Let them alone; they are blind guides. And if the blind lead the blind, both will fall into a pit."

But Peter said to him, "Explain the parable to us."

And he said, "Are you also still without understanding? Do you not see that whatever goes into the mouth passes into the stomach and is expelled? But what comes out of the mouth proceeds from the heart, and this defiles a person. For out of the heart come evil thoughts, murder, adultery, sexual immorality, theft, false witness, slander. These are what defile a person. But to eat with unwashed hands does not defile anyone."

**Interpretation:**

"Defilement" happens all the time in the stock market.

Did you ever buy or sell a share on the basis of a 'hot tip' or rumor? This "hot tip" could be from a salesman paid to recommend the stock so that the company can raise money by dumping stocks on gullible investors.

Many investors have lost millions of dollars each year chasing "hot tips" or believing in market rumors. There are plenty of people or sources who are ready to feed you with BS.

There are some market sources who urge you to buy or sell a particular stock or other security. Their aim is to manipulate the stock price to benefit the person or his other partners in crime. Don't fall a prey to such activities nor be a participant. It's unethical and illegal. Your action could cause scores of investors lose their shirts and you in jeopardy.

Then there are other scam artists who short a stock and then use the social media to spread lies about how the company is soon going to face major problems. When the stock drops, the short sellers cover their positions for a big profit.

View any unsolicited e-mails, letters or phone calls from people you don't know with suspicion.

**Bottom Line:**

**1:** Beware of rumors and tips. There's usually some ulterior motive behind market rumors or tips.

**2:** Don't be a prey to such rumors.

**3:** Don't spread false information in the stock market to manipulate a stock. It's unethical and illegal.

# 35- Fake Stock Market Gurus I

## The Blind Leading the Blind

### Luke 6:39-42

Can a blind man lead a blind man? Will they not both fall into a pit? A disciple is not above his teacher, but everyone when he is fully trained will be like his teacher.

Why do you see the speck that is in your brother's eye, but do not notice the log that is in your own eye? How can you say to your brother, "Brother, let me take out the speck that is in your eye," when you yourself do not see the log that is in your own eye?

You hypocrite, first take the log out of your own eye, and then you will see clearly to take out the speck that is in your brother's eye.

**Interpretation:**

The stock market swarms with rumors and false prophets. You will find scores of experts spouting half-baked wisdom on the movement of stocks. Are these so called experts not similar to the blind man leading a blind man in above parable? Don't listen to such experts or invest on tips. Do your own research. If you need to listen to an expert, then check out his track record. If his recommendations have more hits than misses in the past then start small.

**Bottom Line:**

**1:** Take expert predictions with a grain of salt. Some of them are salesmen paid to recommend the stock so that the company can raise money by dumping stocks on gullible investors.

**2:** These "blind" guys are paid to predict, and they have to "see" what others don't.

**3:** Stay away from stock market pundits making "sure shot" predictions. If they are so sure of their predictions why aren't they putting their money where their mouth is?

# 36- Fake Stock Market Gurus II

## The Tree and Its Fruits

### Matthew 7:15-20

Beware of false prophets, who come to you in sheep's clothing but inwardly are ravenous wolves. You will know them by their fruits. Are grapes gathered from thorns, or figs from thistles? So, every sound tree bears good fruit, but the bad tree bears evil fruit. A sound tree cannot bear evil fruit, nor can a bad tree bear good fruit. Every tree that does not bear good fruit is cut down and thrown into the fire. Thus you will know them by their fruits.

**Interpretation:**

Jesus warned us of false rumors and unscrupulous people, in parables 34 and 35.

Let's now talk about the stock market prognosticators or prophets. These guys have made it a part of their business to forecast the markets. Some of them proclaim to be the best forecasters on the field. It's a pity they are wrong most of the time. Following their advice could have you miss out on a lot of gains.

Nobody can forecast the market accurately. The market is run by emotions which can't be quantified. You will need to know the emotional quotient of all the participants to make a guess.

That's not going to happen. It's time you stopped listening to these false prophets.

Don't bother about market moves. Do your research. Identify good companies. Buy their stocks and hold on to them for a long time. Good stocks are able to weather any storm that comes their way.

Don't panic if there's a temporary correction or the entire market is sliding downwards. Sell stocks if there's a serious problem brewing with the company.

**Bottom Line:**

**1:** Nobody can predict the market well.

**2:** Turn a deaf ear to these false prophets.

# 37- Beware of Scam Artists

## The Good Samaritan

### Luke 10:25-42

On one occasion, a lawyer stood up to test Jesus. "Teacher," he asked, "what must I do to inherit eternal life?"

Jesus asked him, "What is written in the law? What is your reading of it?"

The lawyer replied, "Love the Lord, with all your heart; with your mind, body and soul and love your neighbor as yourself."

"You have answered correctly," Jesus replied. "Do this and you will live."

But the lawyer was not satisfied, so he asked Jesus, "And who is my neighbor?"

In reply, Jesus said, "A man was going down from Jerusalem to Jericho, when he was accosted by robbers. They stripped him of his clothes, beat him and went away, leaving him half dead. A priest happened to be going down the same road, and when he saw the man, he passed by on the other side. So too, a Levite, when he came to the place and saw him, passed by on the other side.

But a Samaritan, as he traveled, came where the man was; and when he saw him, he took pity on him. He went to him and bandaged his wounds, pouring on oil and wine. Then he put the man on his own donkey, took him to an inn and took care of him. The next day he took out two silver coins and gave them to the innkeeper. "Look after him," he said, "and when I return, I will reimburse you for any extra expense you may have."

With these words the Samaritan went away.

Jesus inquired, "Which of these three do you think was a neighbor to the man who fell into the hands of robbers?"

The lawyer replied, "The one who had mercy on him."

Jesus told him, "Go and do likewise."

**Interpretation:**

You will find quite a few Samaritans prowling about you. Learn to recognize them and stay away.

**Stock Market:** View any unsolicited e-mails, letters or phone calls from people you don't know with suspicion. These guys usually arrange webinars or hangouts where they will talk about their rags to riches story. Pay attention to their sob stories-

*Initially these guys were dirt poor. One day, after many, many months of toil and spending thousands of dollars they stumbled upon an awesome discovery which turned them into instant millionaires.* Now these Samaritans want you to be rich? They are willing to part with their secret for only $ 49.99 because if they gave it to you free, you wouldn't value it.

Why would a stranger pick you out to make you rich? Does that make any sense? Why would anyone want to sell an awesome get-rich-quick trading system, with promises to make you an overnight millionaire, for a small fee? Yeah! These Good Samaritans want everybody to be rich! Go ahead, get suckered.

**Easy Money:** If you get a call from a person who professes to help you to raise thousands of dollars for your business provided you sign up and pay up fees, don't jump with joy. He will be a smooth talker. He will not bother to ask you about your business or credit worthiness. After you pay up, this guy vanishes.

You have joined the group of fools who got ripped off by pay-small-fees- to- get- large- sums- of- money scam.

**Fake Property Investments:** "Welcome to my "Get Rich with Properties" or "Make Money from Properties" seminar, buy my e-books or tapes and learn my secrets," said the fake property investment guru to the greedy victim. All these could cost anything from $9.99 to $299.99 depending on what is offered. You eagerly sign up, pay up the fees and attend the seminar or purchase their books or tapes.

You will get a lot of motivational talk and issues which you would have got on the Net for free. No get-rich-quick secrets!

There goes your dream of owning that million dollars property for a song!

**Nigerian scams:** These scams first started from Nigeria and now they can be from any place in the world. You will receive a text message or email offering you a large sum of money the scam artist allegedly wants to transfer out of his country. The crooks will tell you a sob story about money trapped in central banks during civil wars or coups, often in countries currently in the news. Or they may tell you about massive inheritances that are difficult to access because of government restrictions or taxes in the scam artist's country.

Now's the interesting part- You want them to transfer the money to your bank account? No problem. Give them your bank account details, pay fees or charges, which will keep on increasing as you pay them, to help release or transfer the money to your bank account.

Kiss your money and dreams of fabulous wealth goodbye! The con men or the Good Samaritans have vanished with your money.

**Bottom Line:**

**1:** If you fall a prey to the scam artist's schemes and lose money, you will realize they were not the good Samaritans. They were robbers disguised as Samaritans.

**2:** Don't trust anybody. Don't be greedy. Always check the facts before taking a decision.

**3:** Buying or investing in property is a costly business. Talk to genuine industry experts like realtors and builders.

**4:** Not everyone is a fake. There are also genuine Good Samaritans. These guys usually don't promise you instant riches or miracles. Do they have verifiable sources that will vouch for them? Do your homework.

# 38- Trust No One

## The Shrewd Manager

### Luke 16:1-9

There was a rich man whose manager was accused of wasting his possessions. So he called him in and asked him, "What is this I hear about you? Turn in the account of your management, for you can no longer be manager." The manager thought out aloud, "What shall I do now? My master is taking away my job. I am not strong enough to dig, and I am ashamed to beg. I have decided what to do, so that when I am removed from this job, people may receive me into their houses."

So he called in each one of his master's debtors. He asked the first, "How much do you owe my master?" He replied, "Eight hundred gallons of olive oil." The manager told him, "Take your bill, sit down quickly, and make it four hundred."

Then he asked the second, "And how much do you owe?" He replied, "A thousand bushels of wheat." The manager told him, "Take your bill and make it eight hundred."

The master observed what was happening and commended the dishonest manager for his shrewdness. For the sons of this world are shrewder in dealing with their own generation than the sons of light.

And I tell you, make friends for yourselves by means of unrighteous wealth, so that when it fails they may receive you into the eternal dwellings.

One who is faithful in a very little is also faithful in much, and one who is dishonest in a very little is also dishonest in much. If then you have not been faithful in the unrighteous wealth, who will entrust to you the true riches?

And if you have not been faithful in that which is another's, who will give you that which is your own?

No servant can serve two masters, for either he will hate the one and love the other, or he will be devoted to the one and despise the other. You cannot serve God and money.'

**Interpretation and Bottom Line:**

This parable joins the list of Jesus' least understood parables. I am sure you must be wondering why the rich man is commending the dishonest manager who has ripped him off. Apparently, Jesus is trying to tell us that we need to be street-smart, like the dishonest manager, if we need to succeed.

Be on guard. Be smarter (shrewder) than your broker or financial advisor. Trust no one. If your broker or portfolio manager (the shrewd manager) has engaged in unauthorized transactions or other serious misconduct act quickly (see next parable).

# 39- Unscrupulous Brokers and Financial Advisors

## The Unmerciful Servant

### Matthew 18:23-34

Peter came to Jesus and asked, "Lord, how many times shall I forgive my brother when he sins against me? Seven times?"

Jesus answered, "I tell you, not seven times, but seventy-seven times. Therefore, the kingdom of heaven is like a king who wanted to settle accounts with his servants. As he began the settlement, a man who owed him ten thousand talents was brought to him. Since he was not able to pay, the master ordered that he and his wife and his children and all that he had be sold to repay the debt."

The servant fell on his knees before him and assured his master that he would pay back as soon as possible. The servant's master took pity on him, canceled the debt and let him go.

But when that servant went out, he found one of his fellow servants owed him a hundred talents. He grabbed him and began to choke him and demanded to be paid back what he owed. His fellow servant fell to his knees and begged him to be patient and that he would pay him shortly. But he refused. Instead, he went off and had the man thrown into prison until he could pay the debt.

When the other servants saw what had happened, they were greatly distressed and went and told their master everything that had happened.

The master called the servant in. "You wicked servant!" he said, "I canceled all that debt of yours because you begged me to. Shouldn't you have had mercy on your fellow servant just as I had on you?"

In anger, his master turned him over to the jailers to be tortured, until he paid back all he owed."

**Interpretation:**

There are honest brokers and financial advisors and then there are the unscrupulous. I am going to assume that you were unfortunate to employ the services of an unscrupulous / fraudulent broker or financial advisor.

If you think you have a justifiable dispute against your broker or advisor then you need to take action quickly. If you lick your wounds in silence, then these individuals will continue to rip off other unsuspecting investors.

**How do you file a complaint?**

If your complaint is against a stockbroker, you need to file a dispute with either the Securities and Exchange Commission (SEC) http://www.sec.gov/investor/brokers.htm or FINRA (**www.finra.org**).

If your complaint is against a Certified Financial Planner (CFP), you can file with the **Certified Financial Planner Board of Standards**.

If it is against a Chartered Financial Analyst (CFA), you can contact the **Association of Investment and Research.**

Contact the division of your state or provincial securities commission that handles complaints against brokers, advisors and financial planners.

If these options don't work, your final course of action is to take legal action.

**Bottom Line:**

**1:** The best way to avoid unscrupulous or fraudulent brokers or advisors is to check the background of the firm and broker or planner for any disciplinary problems in the past. You also should check to see whether they are registered or licensed.

**2:** If you do business with an unregistered securities broker or a firm that cheats on you or goes out of business, there may be no way for you to recover your money.

**3:** Check out the **Central Registration Depository** (CRD), http://www.sec.gov/answers/crd.htm, a computerized database that contains information about most brokers, their representatives, and the firms they work for.

**4:** To find out about an investment adviser and whether it is properly registered, read its registration form, called '**Form ADV**.' You can view an adviser's most recent Form ADV online by visiting the **Investment Adviser Public Disclosure (IAPD)** website. http://www.adviserinfo.sec.gov/IAPD/Content/IapdMain/iapd_SiteMap.aspx

**5:** If you plan to do business with a brokerage firm, you should find out whether the brokerage firm and its clearing firm are members of the **Securities Investor Protection Corporation** (SIPC). http://www.sec.gov/answers/sipc.htm

**6:** Check out the SEC website
http://www.sec.gov/investor/brokers.htm for more details.

**7:** If you don't understand an investment which your broker or advisor suggests, say so. An honest broker or advisor will always ensure that you fully understand an investment beforehand.

**8:** Losing money on an investment doesn't mean you can sue your advisor for bad advice. There's no law or regulation which say that investors are guaranteed a return!

**9:** Markets are risky by nature and you must be prepared to take on some risk when you invest.

**10:** If you feel you have a legitimate dispute with your broker or advisor, then you should file a complaint with the regulators or the charter organizations to which your broker or advisor belongs.

**11:** Contact the division of your state or provincial securities commission that handles complaints against brokers, advisors and financial planners.

**12:** If nothing works, hire an attorney.

# 40- The Internet Is Your Friend

## Friend in Need

### Luke 11:5-8

Suppose one of you has a friend, and he comes to your place at midnight and says, "Friend, lend me three loaves of bread, because a friend of mine on a journey has come to visit me, and I have nothing to set before him." What would you reply? I am sure you will say, "Don't bother me. The door is already locked, and my children are with me in bed. I can't get up and give you anything." I tell you, though you will not get up and give him anything because he is your friend, yet because of his impudence you will rise and give him whatever he needs. Ask, and it will be given to you; seek, and you will find; knock and the door will be opened to you. Remember this always.

**Interpretation:**

Do you have a friend who will help and advise you 24/7 without a word of protest?

The Internet!

If you have doubts about any company, stock or investment you own, you can always Google the information you seek. Check the facts on the Net before you take an investment decision.

Here are the pick of the best and most popular sites for stocks on the Net today. They provide stock market quotes, information or tools which you will need for your analysis.

Yahoo Finance, Google Finance, Morningstar, SmartMoney, Investors.com, Bloomberg.com, NYSE, The Motley Fool, CNN/Money , About.com, Stocks, StockCharts.com, Reuters - News on Top Stocks , CBS MarketWatch, Daily Stocks

**Bottom Line:**

The Net is a source of good as well as bad information about stocks, the stock market and investing.

You need to be careful while accessing a site for the required information. Stick to sites like those given above.

# Summary

Here's a synopsis of what we learned about investing from these parables-

**1: The Rich Young Man-** Greed is the first deadly sin of investing. Greed rules the market. Greed is one of the main causes of financial crises and wars over the centuries. What are the symptoms of greed? You need to learn to control this emotion if you want to be rich.

**2: Ten Servants and Minas-** Don't stash your cash under the mattress. Inflation will erode the value of your money, if you do so. Invest wisely. Make your money race past the rate of inflation.

**3: The Workers in the Vineyard-** It's the quality of the stock and the price you buy it that determines whether you will be very rich or not. With one home run investment a late bloomer can become rich in a flash. You could beat the guys who have been holding on to mediocre stocks for years.

**4: The Ten Virgins-** Don't be like the foolish virgins. If you have a cushion of cash, it can help you stay invested when stocks fall during bearish periods.

**5: Lowest Seat at a Feast-** Start small. After your position turns profitable, scale up.

**6: Hidden Treasure and Priceless Pearl-** If your homework or a most reliable source tells you that a particular stock will shoot up soon, buy all the stock which you can afford with a trailing stop loss. Sell your existing investments, if necessary, to buy this stock.

**7: The Eagles and the Carcass-** Be a value investor. Buy when the market is littered with battered stocks of good companies and everybody is selling.

**8: Faithful and Wise Servant-** As a company shareholder or mutual fund investor know your rights.

**9: The Shepherd and His Flock-** Don't be a passive investor. You might be taken for a ride by brokers and financial advisors who are more interested in collecting their fees and commissions rather than the performance of your portfolio.

**10: The Growing Seed-** Historically, small caps have outperformed the large caps over long periods of time. Picking the right small cap stocks can grow your wealth over a period of time.

**11: The Ten Lepers-** If you have identified a great company and bought its shares. Hold on to the shares for at least 5 to 10 years and you will be rewarded.

**12: The Wise and Foolish Builders-** Keep stocks of companies with strong foundations in your portfolio.

**13: Lamp on a Stand-** Great companies don't remain hidden for long. It's a matter of time before some astute investor or analyst tracks them down and exposes them to the world.

**14: The Two Debtors-** Invest in stocks of shareholder friendly companies. These companies realize that they will have loyal shareholders if the company treats them well.

**15: Four Types of Soil-** Learn to identify the characteristics of your company before taking an investment decision.

**16: Lazarus and the Rich Man-** The stock market is ruled by cycles. What goes up (bullish trend) has to come down (bearish trend) after a while.

**17: The Weather Signs-** The stock market is unpredictable and uncontrollable. Market gurus and experts go to great lengths to try to predict the stock market. Some of them are successful for a limited period of time before Mr. Market brings them to their knees.

**18: The Sheep and the Goats-** If an investment or a stock has not fulfilled your investment objectives, sell them quickly. They are doing your portfolio no good.

**19: The Barren Fig Tree-** Don't hold to underperformers for long rationalizing they will rise and cover your losses. The losses will only escalate. It's time to move on to better stocks.

**20: The Two Sons-** If you have made a mistake, accept it and get out of a losing position quickly. You might be saddled with a huge loss, if you don't.

**21: The Evil Tenants of the Vineyard-** Derivatives and 'Averaging Down' strategy are like the evil tenants of the vineyard.

**22: Old Cloth and New Wine / Wineskins-** Whether you are a company or an individual investor, you need to adapt to the changing scenario or wither. Be nimble enough to get out of a losing position quickly. Don't try to patch up your mistakes with more cash infusion.

**23: Watchfulness-** Be vigilant and informed about your portfolio; your debt and finances; the financial markets, and the general economy to help you face the unforeseen surprises or shocks which the market will throw on your lap.

**24: Signs from a Fig Tree-** Be alert. Keep a watch over stock market trends, global news, adverse company and economic news. If there is a sudden reversal you will be in a position to take immediate corrective action.

**25: Master and Servant-** Humility, patience and discipline are the hallmarks of a wise and successful investor.

**26: The Rich Fool-** It's always safer to buy stocks of companies which are fiscally prudent.

**27: The Great Banquet-** If you are a trader and if your position goes against you, liquidate it immediately. Don't try to cover your losses by executing more trades. If your day's not good, you will end up with huge losses.

**28: The Weeds-** Most people go over the edge and sell their profitable shares in panic selling situations. It's a perfect situation for great buying opportunities.

**29: The Fishing Net-** Keep the performers and sell the non-performers from your portfolio.

**30: The Lost Sheep, Lost Coin-** There are many sites which will help you track down your missing or unclaimed money, stocks, IRS tax refunds, Pension and Life insurance.......

**31: The Cost of Being a Disciple-** Invest within your means. Start small if you have very little money to start with. Don't invest using margin money.

**32: The Pharisee and the Tax Collector-** It's difficult to outsmart Mr. Market all the time. Losses are part of the game. Use stop loss to limit your losses. Don't cheat on the IRS.

**33: What Defiles a Person-** Beware of rumors and tips. Don't spread wrong information for self-benefit.

**34: The Doctor and the Sick-** It's impossible to avoid either death or taxes but we can try to minimize our tax burden.

**35: The Blind Leading the Blind-** The stock market swarms with rumors and false prophets. Be wary of stock market pundits making 'definitely going to happen' predictions. If they are so sure of their predictions why aren't they investors?

**36: The Shrewd Manager-** Be Street Smart. If you think you have been ripped by your broker, advisor or a scam artist you need to take action without delay.

**37: The Unmerciful Servant-** Here's how to take action against unscrupulous brokers, scam artists or advisors who have been ripping you off.

**38: The Good Samaritan-** Be wary of the stock market Samaritans. They will pretend to be your friend and promise you great riches. It could be the biggest mistake of your life. Don't trust anybody. Always check the facts before taking a decision.

**39: The Tree and Its Fruits-** The stock market prognosticators have made it a part of their business to forecast the markets. It's a pity that they are wrong most of the time. Following their advice could have you miss out on a lot of gains. It's time you stopped listening to these false prophets and did your own homework.

**40: Friend in Need-** Who is your friend who will help and advise you 24/7 without a word of protest? The Internet is a source of good as well as bad information about stocks, the stock market and investing.

You need to be careful while accessing a site for the required information. Stick to the best and most popular sites for stocks on the Net today.

# Thank You!

Thank you for reading my book. If you enjoyed it, it would be greatly appreciated if you left a review so others can receive the same benefits you have. Your review will help me see what is and isn't working so I can better serve you and all my other readers even more.

Here's the link:

http://www.amazon.com/dp/B00M4767G8

http://ASIN.cc/11ujpiL

Thanks for any help you can provide to get the word out!

# My Books

If you liked this book, you will also love these books. Get them and be enlightened.

**THE 40 PARABLES OF INVESTING**
http://ASIN.cc/11ujpiL
https://www.createspace.com /5029013

**HOW TO BE THE MASTER OF THE UNIVERSE**
http://ASIN.cc/ychKfq
https://www.createspace.com /5034839

**The Secret Gospel of Thomas: Decoded**
http://ASIN.cc/1Y9SQ8W
https://www.createspace.com/5470783

**Game of Illusions**
http://ASIN.cc/ytWryA
https://www.createspace.com /5042255

**Game of Life**
http://ASIN.cc/1Q7_D9W
https://www.createspace.com/5344252

**HOW TO GET ANYTHING YOU WANT? MAKE A MAGICK MIRROR!**
http://ASIN.cc/RahVJf
https://www.createspace.com/5040665

**How to Be Enriched in Every Way**
http://ASIN.cc/12Jo4zL
https://www.createspace.com /5065824

**Betrayer or the Chosen One? Judas Tells His Side**
http://www.amazon.com/dp/B00XGFI1OS
http://ASIN.cc/1ZePUvf

**I CHING OF THE STOCK MARKET**
http://ASIN.cc/bxxqcL
https://www.createspace.com /5069717

**WHY ME?**
http://ASIN.cc/e5qS5f

**THE HARE AND THE TORTOISE -BEAT THE BULLIES!**
http://ASIN.cc/mocBz0

**The Little Book That Beats the Bullies**
http://ASIN.cc/12QD6kW
https://www.createspace.com /5043967

**DATING ADVICE: 30 Frequently Asked Questions**
http://ASIN.cc/V_YBvf

www.ingramcontent.com/pod-product-compliance
Lightning Source LLC
Chambersburg PA
CBHW051807170526
45167CB00005B/1921